To vaness

312 W 2nd St, Casper, WY 82601

This book is a work of nonfiction. Any resemblance to real persons, living or dead, or real events is purely coincidental.

ISBN 979-8-9991577-1-3
First Edition
November 2025
Published by Xiaotun LLC

Table of Contents

CHPTER-1 :
THE FACE TELLS All

CHPTER-3: VOICE & SPEECH SECRETS

CHPTER-4: CONTEXTUAL INSIGHTS

CHPTER-5: READING PEOPLE THROUGH THEIR RESPONSES

CHPTER-6:
RECOGNIZING PERSONALITY TYPES THROUGH BEHAVIOR

Chapter 1

The Face Tells All

Brows and Personality Traits

Our eyebrows do far more than frame our faces — they're one of the most powerful, expressive tools in nonverbal communication. Eyebrows can reveal emotional reactions within milliseconds, signaling surprise, confusion, anger, or joy. But beyond these momentary expressions, research and observation suggest that the shape, movement, and resting position of eyebrows may also offer subtle clues about personality traits and inner emotional patterns. In this article, we explore what your brows might be saying about you — and what others' brows might reveal — through three lenses: reactions to others' success, physical traits linked to decisiveness or sensitivity, and eyebrow placement as an indicator of optimism and energy.

Frown might mean envy your success

You're sharing good news — a promotion, a creative breakthrough, or maybe just a really lucky travel upgrade — and someone across the room frowns. It lasts only a second, perhaps hidden behind a polite smile. But you saw it: a micro-frown, a flicker of tight brows drawn inward.

That fleeting frown might be more than momentary discomfort. **Eyebrow contractions — especially those that briefly appear when good news is shared — are one of the microexpressions most associated with envy.** Unlike anger, which typically causes brows to lower and the eyes to narrow with intensity, envy produces a subtler pattern: **A pinching of the brows, tension around the forehead, and a delay or mismatch in smiling.**

This kind of reaction isn't always malicious. Envy often emerges when someone feels insecure, overlooked, or stuck. That inward brow movement can be a **nonverbal cue of internal conflict**: the person may genuinely like you, but your success unintentionally highlights their dissatisfaction with themselves. It's not always personal — but it is revealing.

People who frequently display this kind of involuntary brow movement in social settings might struggle with **social comparison**, and may be prone to **low self-esteem or impostor syndrome**. If you see it often, it's less about confronting them and more about understanding the quiet tension they carry. In team settings or friendships, it may signal a need for reassurance or inclusion.

Observing women's personality From eyebrow shape

The physical shape and density of eyebrows — whether naturally thick or thin — may also hint at aspects of a person's decision-making style and emotional responsiveness.

Thick eyebrows are often associated with boldness, assertiveness, and strong-willed personalities. People with thick brows are more likely to take decisive action, resist external pressure, and trust their own instincts. Several personality studies and observational psychology reports suggest that **individuals with thick brows tend to score higher on measures of confidence and leadership orientation.** They're often perceived as direct, no-nonsense types — even if their actual behavior is more nuanced.

This doesn't mean people with thick brows are always aggressive or dominant. Rather, they tend to **project authority and self-possession**, which can sometimes be misread as arrogance or coldness. But when paired with expressive movement — like raised brows or frequent arching — thick eyebrows can also communicate warmth and humor.

In contrast, **thin eyebrows** — whether naturally fine or over-plucked — are often associated with **sensitivity, caution, and empathy.** Thin-browed individuals may be more attuned to emotional nuance, and they might second-guess decisions if they worry about how others feel. There's an introspective quality here: **thin eyebrows are often read as a visual metaphor for internal processing,** for emotional softness.

People with thinner brows might avoid conflict, take longer to reach conclusions, or feel anxious under pressure. But they're also more likely to listen, to observe, and to adapt. In group dynamics, they often serve as mediators or emotional barometers.

Of course, brow shape isn't destiny. Grooming habits, fashion trends, and genetics all play a role. But time and again, body language specialists have found that **people tend to express their personalities in how they allow or alter their natural brows.** A person who chooses to emphasize strong, bold brows may be reinforcing an identity of confidence — or compensating for internal uncertainty.

The psychological signals revealed by the state of eyebrow

Take a moment to picture someone with **high-set eyebrows** — those that rest further above the eyes, creating a larger upper eyelid space. What do you imagine? Often, people describe them as **alert, observant, or open-minded.** Now picture **low-set brows**, closer to the eyes, lending a more intense or focused appearance. These individuals are often described as **serious, grounded, or intense.**

This isn't just subjective. Body language experts often interpret **high-set brows** as indicators of **curiosity, optimism, and cognitive openness**. People with higher brows tend to keep more physical distance between their eyes and eyebrows, which creates the appearance of wide-eyed wonder. This correlates with a **personality style that is observant, imaginative, and mentally flexible.** High-set brows often belong to people who pause before reacting — literally and figuratively — giving them a reputation for being calm, tolerant, and big-picture thinkers.

On the other hand, **low-set eyebrows** are linked to **focus, realism, and high mental energy.** These individuals might be quick thinkers, prone to making fast decisions, and often operate in high-efficiency, low-distraction modes. Low-set brows narrow the visual space around the eyes, leading to a **perception of intensity.** These people often give the impression of seriousness or even intimidation, especially when not smiling.

But it's not a matter of good vs bad. High brows may sometimes be perceived as **detached** or lacking urgency. Low brows, while focused, can sometimes be seen as **rigid or too intense**. Like all traits, balance is key.

Importantly, **eyebrow height doesn't change much with age,** though muscle tension and expressions can alter the illusion of height. This means eyebrow placement can serve as a relatively stable nonverbal trait, especially in understanding others' default energy and social approach.

Reading with Empathy

It's easy to overanalyze — to turn every twitch of the brow into a declaration of character. But the truth lies **in patterns**, not moments. One frown doesn't mean envy. One low-set brow doesn't equal rigidity. But **consistent, unconscious expressions can offer insight** into how someone moves through the world.

When we observe carefully, not to judge but to understand, eyebrows become less about surface impressions and more about emotional architecture. A person's brows may quietly say: *I'm proud but afraid, I'm gentle but tired, or I'm happy for you but worried I'm falling behind.*

Brows are subtle storytellers — and when we listen closely, they can help us understand not just others, but ourselves.

Eyes and Hidden Truths

They say the eyes are the windows to the soul — but they're also the mirrors of emotion. Eye movements, eye contact, blink patterns, and even eye shape all contribute to the subtle art of emotional signaling. While the mouth may lie and the body may posture, the eyes are far harder to control. In high-stakes conversations, personal relationships, or professional settings, understanding someone's eyes often tells you more than their words. In this article, we examine three specific eye-related cues — blinking rate, eye contact patterns, and eye size — and how they reflect not just transient emotions, but deep-seated personality traits.

Blinking Rate — Focused or Lying?

Blinking is one of the most overlooked nonverbal cues — and also one of the most revealing. We blink for physiological reasons (to lubricate the eyes), but the rate and rhythm of blinking can shift dramatically depending on our mental state, emotional intensity, or even our intent to deceive.

In general, lower blink rates are associated with high concentration. When people are deeply focused — reading, solving a problem, listening intently — they blink less. This is often seen in competitive environments: a chess player staring at the board, a job candidate trying to absorb a question, or an athlete awaiting a signal. The body conserves movement, and the blink rate slows to prioritize visual input.

On the other hand, a sudden increase in blink rate may signal stress, anxiety, or cognitive overload. It can also be a red flag during deception. Studies in deception detection have found that people often blink more frequently when they are fabricating information or trying to maintain a false impression. This is not because blinking itself is a lie, but because lying creates internal tension and higher cognitive load, which leaks through the body.

But here's where interpretation gets tricky. High blinking doesn't always mean someone is lying — it could mean they're nervous, excited, or emotionally stirred. For example, someone on a first date may blink rapidly simply due to arousal or self-consciousness, not dishonesty.

Context is everything. Consistent, evenly spaced blinks suggest calm engagement. Sudden shifts — a drop followed by a flurry — often indicate that something internal just changed:

an emotional reaction, a shift in truthfulness, or a spike in pressure.

And here's a subtle but telling clue: **If someone blinks a lot around you, they may be silently judging you.** Blinking becomes more frequent when the brain is actively evaluating, measuring, or even criticizing — especially in high-stakes social encounters.

If you're watching closely, blinking tells a story. Not in words — but in timing.

Eye Contact That Unmasks True Emotions

Eye contact is a powerful form of social connection. It can invite trust, command respect, convey vulnerability, or expose insecurity — often all within a few seconds. Yet eye contact is more complex than simply "looking someone in the eye." It's a dynamic exchange that reveals how someone feels about themselves, about you, and about the moment you're sharing.

Genuine emotional connection is often marked by sustained, soft eye contact. It's not a stare — it's a steady gaze that flows with conversation. People who are comfortable with intimacy, empathy, and authenticity tend to maintain eye contact more naturally, allowing their emotions to be seen.

Conversely, avoiding eye contact can signal discomfort — but the reason varies. Some people avert their gaze when they're shy, anxious, or uncertain. Others avoid eye contact as a defense mechanism, afraid of being emotionally exposed. In some cases, lack of eye contact can signal deception, especially when it appears in contrast to otherwise confident behavior.

There's also a difference between eye contact and eye intensity. A person can look you in the eye while still masking emotion — particularly if they maintain eye contact with too much force or stillness. **If someone stares at you for too long, it's not intimacy — it's aggression, especially if they're a stranger.** This type of gaze often functions less as connection and more as a challenge, a way of asserting dominance or testing boundaries.

Prolonged, unblinking stares may signal manipulation, dominance, or rehearsed performance. In such cases, the eye contact isn't about connection — it's about control.

Interestingly, micro-expressions in the eyes can betray the truth even when someone is trying to hide it. For example:

- A brief widening of the eyes may show surprise or fear.
- A sudden narrowing can indicate suspicion or anger.
- A delayed blink after emotional news may suggest suppression.

When you sense a mismatch — someone's words say one thing,

but their eyes flicker or freeze — trust the eyes. They tend to tell the story the mouth won't.

Eye Size and Personality: Expressive or Reserved?

While eye size is largely a genetic feature, the perceived size of the eyes — especially when animated in conversation — can suggest personality traits, emotional openness, or social comfort.

Larger, more expressive eyes tend to be associated with openness, warmth, and emotional sensitivity. People whose eyes appear wide or round when speaking often project a sense of innocence, empathy, or artistic sensitivity. In personality psychology, this aligns with higher scores on traits like agreeableness and emotional expressiveness.

It's not just biology — it's behavior. People who widen their eyes during storytelling, who raise their brows often, or who "smile with their eyes" are generally more attuned to emotional dynamics. They use their faces — especially the eyes — as instruments of connection.

By contrast, people with smaller or more reserved eye expressions may come across as more stoic, cautious, or introspective. This doesn't mean they lack emotion — only that they don't externalize it as freely. In fact, such individuals are often seen as emotionally resilient, self-contained, or highly rational. Their eyes may remain still during conversations, with minimal flicker or widening, and they may blink slowly or infrequently.

Cultural norms play a role, too. In many East Asian cultures, restraint in eye expression is viewed as respectful, while in Western cultures, emotional openness is often expected through facial cues. What one group sees as sincere, another may perceive as exaggerated.

Over time, habitual facial expressions can subtly reshape the perception of eye size. Those who frequently express surprise, joy, or openness may appear to have larger eyes due to raised brows and lifted lids. Those who often squint or narrow their gaze may give the impression of smaller, more guarded eyes — even if the anatomical size hasn't changed.

Ultimately, eye size cues us into how freely someone experiences and shares their internal world. Wide eyes welcome you in. Narrowed eyes keep the boundary. But neither is better — they simply reflect different emotional styles.

Looks to Their Left, They Are Recalling Memories

When someone's eyes shift to their left while speaking, it often reflects the brain's process of retrieving stored information. In observational psychology, this movement is commonly linked to memory recall — reaching into the past to access real experiences, sounds, or images.

During conversation, you might notice this subtle glance when someone answers questions like "What did you see?" or "How did it happen?" The eyes may move left and sometimes slightly down, signaling that the mind is replaying something it has already recorded.

This doesn't mean it's an infallible truth detector. Stress, personal habits, and even handedness can influence the direction of gaze. However, in natural, relaxed dialogue, a consistent leftward glance often suggests the speaker is remembering rather than inventing.

Observers sometimes describe it as watching someone "rewind" their mental tape. The shift pairs well with other cues — a thoughtful pause, softening facial muscles, or a slight nostalgic smile can reinforce the sense of genuine recollection.

Understanding this subtle signal helps you better read cognitive processing. A look to the left isn't just eye movement; it's a window into the brain's archive, where past experiences are brought back into the present moment.

Looks to The Right, Means They Are Processing Thoughts

When a person's eyes move to their right during conversation, it is often associated with active mental construction. Instead of pulling from the past, the brain may be piecing together new ideas, imagining scenarios, or formulating responses. This movement is frequently seen when people are asked to create, speculate, or solve problems on the spot.

In everyday dialogue, you might notice this rightward glance when someone is asked "What could happen if...?" or "How would you explain...?" The eyes shift as the mind assembles possibilities rather than recalling a fixed memory.

This doesn't indicate deception by itself. Creative thinking naturally requires "building" images or words, so the rightward gaze can simply signal imagination at work. Skilled communicators watch for patterns: if the glance pairs with longer pauses or upward movement of the brows, it often marks active cognitive processing.

Unlike the leftward "memory look," the rightward movement feels forward-looking, as if the mind is sketching something that doesn't yet exist. It's a moment where internal thought is visible through a small, unconscious gesture.

Recognizing this cue allows deeper understanding of mental

activity. A glance to the right is not about recalling what has been, but shaping what could be — a silent indicator of the brain in creation mode.

Final Glance:
Seeing the Signals Behind the Eyes

Eyes are always moving — even when we don't notice. They blink, shift, scan, and settle. In those tiny movements lies a hidden language, one that reveals far more than our practiced speech.

- Rapid blinking may whisper stress — or a cover story.
- Sustained eye contact may invite trust — or mask control.
- Animated, expressive eyes may say, "Come closer." Reserved ones might say, "Proceed with care."
- And remember: **If someone stares at you for too long, especially if they're a stranger, they're not showing affection — they're showing aggression.**

The art of reading eyes isn't about judging — it's about noticing. We all send signals we don't intend. And we all appreciate being seen — truly seen — beneath the surface.

So next time you're in conversation, look beyond the words. Look at the rhythm, the gaze, the blink. Because sometimes, what someone's eyes say in one second is more honest than what their mouth can say in a minute.

Nose and Psychological Signals

The nose is often overlooked in body language analysis, dismissed as too subtle or too fixed to reveal much. But in truth, **the nose plays a surprisingly expressive role in nonverbal communication**, particularly when it comes to **self-perception, social discomfort, emotional aversion, and internal status.** While it doesn't move as dramatically as the eyes or hands, the nose — through gesture, tension, or even its shape — can reveal emotional micro-shifts and personality patterns. In this article, we examine three key aspects of nasal communication: the **scrunch** that signals disgust or disdain, the touch that may suggest deception or discomfort, and how the bridge height may silently reflect confidence and social role.

Nose Scrunching: Decoding Disgust and Disdain

One of the clearest emotional expressions involving the nose is the scrunch — that quick wrinkling of the bridge, often paired with a slight lift of the upper lip. It may last just a second, but it sends a loud message: **something is unpleasant, repulsive, or beneath one's standards.**

In emotional psychology, **nose scrunching is closely tied to the expression of disgust**, one of the basic universal emotions identified by Paul Ekman and others. It's a primitive reaction, originally linked to avoiding bad smells or contaminated substances. But in modern life, we scrunch our noses **not only at physical odors but also at moral, social, or psychological "contaminants."**

For example, a person might scrunch their nose:

- Upon hearing someone boast excessively
- When watching someone behave rudely in public
- In response to a political opinion they find offensive

In these cases, the nose movement signals **disdain rather than pure disgust**. It reflects **moral distancing**: "I don't want this near me — not just physically, but ideologically."
In social dynamics, frequent nose scrunching can mark

someone as **judgmental, sensitive to social norms, or easily repulsed.** On the positive side, it may indicate **strong personal values and boundaries.** On the negative side, it may reflect **rigidity or an aversion to differing viewpoints.**

This subtle cue is also important in decoding relationships. If someone scrunches their nose **at another person**, even momentarily, it could indicate **a break in respect or connection.** It's worth noting who triggers it — and how often.

Touching the Nose — A Sign of Discomfort or Deception?

Among all body language gestures, **touching the nose** has perhaps one of the most debated meanings. Popular psychology books often claim it's a sign someone is lying — and while this isn't universally true, **it can be a red flag when combined with other cues.**

Let's break it down.

When people feel anxious, self-conscious, or guilty, they tend to perform **self-soothing gestures** — touching the face, rubbing the neck, playing with jewelry, or adjusting clothing. The nose, rich with nerve endings and connected to both emotional and physical sensitivity, often becomes a focal point. A person might:

Rub the side of the nose quickly

Scratch near the nostrils

Pinch the bridge of the nose during thought

According to research in nonverbal behavior, **nose-touching increases under emotional stress or when someone feels they're being scrutinized.** This includes during interviews, interrogations, or emotionally loaded conversations. In these situations, the gesture may signal **discomfort, not necessarily deception.**

However, in deception research, one explanation is physiological: **lying can stimulate a small release of adrenaline,** which may cause **a tingling or itching sensation** in the nose. The brain, recognizing the discomfort, leads the person to touch or rub the area — often unconsciously. This is why **nose-touching is sometimes correlated with dishonesty**, particularly when it appears alongside:

- Inconsistent verbal responses
- Avoidant eye contact
- Excessive justification

That said, not everyone who touches their nose is lying. Some people do it habitually, or as a concentration aid. Others may be nervous or simply have allergies.

The key is **context and clusters.** If nose-touching occurs in **combination with verbal hesitation, fidgeting, or emotional withdrawal,** it's more likely to indicate internal conflict — which could stem from deception, but also from fear, shame, or uncertainty.

In short, **the nose touch doesn't scream "lie" — but it often whispers "something's not right."**

Nose Bridge Height: Confidence and Social Status

Unlike fleeting expressions or gestures, the **structure of the nose,** particularly the **height and prominence of the nasal bridge,** may convey longer-term traits related to self-perception, identity, and social energy.

A **high nasal bridge** — where the nose appears more pronounced in profile and forms a strong, straight line from the brow — is often **unconsciously associated with confidence, status, and authority.** Historically, prominent noses were idealized in art and sculpture to symbolize **strength, nobility, and leadership.** Think of Roman busts, Renaissance portraits, or modern fashion photography.

While these associations are cultural and not biologically deterministic, they influence how people are perceived — and how they **see themselves.**

Studies in facial trait attribution show that individuals with high nasal bridges are often rated as:

- More dominant
- More intelligent
- Less emotionally expressive

This perception may shape behavior. People who grow up receiving feedback that they appear "strong" or "serious" may internalize these roles, becoming more assertive or emotionally restrained over time.

Conversely, a **lower nasal bridge** — where the nose appears flatter or more softly contoured — may be associated with **approachability, warmth, or modesty.** These individuals are often perceived as **less intimidating and more emotionally available.** In some cultures, this look aligns with ideals of humility and friendliness rather than command.

It's important to emphasize: **bridge height does not determine character**, but it can shape **social perception**, which in turn influences **self-perception**. A person viewed as "authoritative" may begin to behave more confidently, just as someone seen as "gentle" may downplay assertiveness, even if they're capable of it.

Interestingly, individuals who alter the structure of their nose through surgery often report shifts in self-image and confidence. The nose, as a central feature of the face, acts as a psychological anchor for identity.

Final Thoughts: A Face-Centered Mirror

The nose might seem like a passive facial feature — fixed, unmoving, unremarkable. But it **reacts, signals, and reveals** more than we think.

- A scrunched nose reveals our **moral disgust**, not just our distaste.
- A sudden nose touch hints at **emotional tension** — perhaps even a hidden truth.
- And the bridge of the nose, sculpted by genetics or choice, becomes a **symbol of how we carry ourselves socially.**

Like all body language, nasal cues must be read with care — in clusters, in context, and without assumption. But when we learn to notice them, we begin to see more clearly not just what someone is doing, but **how they feel about themselves and the moment they're in.**

In the theater of the face, the nose may not have the leading role — but it's delivering quiet lines that matter.

Reading a Person's Emotions through Their Lips

Among all facial features, the mouth is arguably the most expressive — both verbally and nonverbally. We use it to speak, to smile, to frown, and to convey countless emotions without saying a single word. But beyond speech, the **micro-behaviors of the mouth — tension, movement, and form — often signal our inner emotional states and social tendencies.** In this article, we explore how three distinct mouth cues — pressed lips, lip licking, and lip shape — reflect deeper truths about how we communicate, regulate emotion, and connect with others.

Pressed Lips: The Silent Signal of Hidden Anger

One of the most telling signs of emotional restraint is the

pressed-lip expression — lips drawn together in a tight, thin line, often with the corners turned slightly downward. It's a subtle, quiet gesture that usually appears **when someone is holding something back.**

In nonverbal communication, **pressed lips are a classic signal of suppressed anger, disapproval, or frustration.** The tighter the lips, the greater the internal pressure. This gesture often happens unconsciously, as the body attempts to **literally "seal in" an emotion that feels dangerous or inappropriate to express.**

You might see pressed lips when:

- A colleague disagrees but chooses not to speak up
- A partner is hurt but unwilling to start a conflict
- A person receives criticism they don't agree with

The message is simple but powerful: *"I'm not okay — but I'm not going to say it."*

What's critical here is **context and duration.** A brief lip press may indicate momentary hesitation or thoughtfulness. But sustained or repeated pressing often means **long-term emotional tension or relational strain.** In close relationships, it may precede emotional withdrawal or passive-aggressive behavior. In professional settings, it can signal **a breakdown in open communication.**

Pressed lips can also reflect **self-restraint** — the effort to stay professional, calm, or diplomatic in difficult moments. While this may be socially appropriate, overuse of this emotional suppression can create long-term stress and resentment.

Ultimately, the pressed mouth is a red flag: **the words aren't being said, but the emotion is still there — tightly sealed but fully alive.**

Lip Licking: Physical Manifestation of Anxiety

Another often-overlooked cue is **lip licking** — a quick swipe of the tongue across the lips, often done automatically and without awareness. While it may seem like a harmless habit, it's actually a strong indicator of **nervous energy and internal discomfort.**

Lip licking increases when we experience:

- **Anxiety or uncertainty**
- **Fear of judgment**
- **Social self-consciousness**
- **Dehydration caused by adrenaline**

Here's what happens physiologically: **When the body enters a stress state**, even a mild one (like being put on the spot or asked a difficult question), the fight-or-flight system activates. One of its subtler effects is **drying of the mouth**, due to reduced saliva production. In response, people often lick their lips — not because they want to draw attention, but because **the body is trying to restore balance.**

However, repeated lip licking — especially in high-pressure or evaluative settings — may send **nonverbal signals of vulnerability**. It can indicate **lack of confidence**, discomfort with the current topic, or fear of saying the wrong thing. Some individuals also develop this as a **self-soothing mechanism** — a way to manage anxiety through small, repetitive motions.

In interviews, negotiations, or public speaking, excessive lip licking may undermine perceived credibility, even if the speaker is competent. It doesn't mean they lack ability — just that **their body is revealing an inner tension they may not yet have mastered.**

On the other hand, occasional lip licking — paired with eye contact and a steady tone — might simply reflect **a thoughtful pause** or **physical dryness**. As always, the meaning becomes clear when read in clusters.

The takeaway? **If someone's words seem confident, but their mouth is restless, it's the mouth you should trust.**

Full vs Thin Lips: Warmth or Reserve?

Unlike lip movement, **lip shape** is largely structural — we're born with it. But over time, the **perception of lip fullness or thinness** has come to symbolize deeper emotional and social traits in both popular psychology and interpersonal judgment. **Full lips** are often associated with:

- Emotional openness
- Expressiveness
- Nurturing qualities
- High sociability

People with naturally full lips tend to be **perceived as warm, empathetic, and responsive.** This is especially true in cultures where lip fullness is idealized as a sign of sensuality, vitality, or feminine energy. In personality profiling, full lips are sometimes correlated with **high agreeableness and extraversion,** and individuals with this feature may be more likely to speak emotionally, show affection openly, and seek connection.

However, full lips can also lead to **expectations of emotional availability,** whether or not the person feels comfortable with that. In social dynamics, they may be misread as "soft" or overly romantic, even when the person is logical or guarded internally.

In contrast, **thin lips** are commonly linked to:

- Restraint
- Precision
- Emotional reserve
- Independence

Individuals with thinner lips may be **seen as more self-contained, analytical, or serious**, often favoring clarity over emotional elaboration. They may not easily show affection through words or facial expressions — not because they lack depth, but because they tend to **process emotion internally.**

In the workplace, people with thin lips are sometimes misjudged as cold or aloof — but many are simply **selective in how and when they connect.** They often prioritize loyalty and depth over breadth in relationships.

That said, **lip shape isn't destiny.** Grooming habits (e.g., overlining, cosmetic enhancement), posture, and expression can all shift the perception of lip fullness. A thin-lipped person who smiles often may still be read as warm. A full-lipped person with a flat affect may still come across as distant.

In short: **full lips may invite emotional access,** while **thin lips may create emotional boundaries.** Neither is better — they simply reflect different communication rhythms.

Mouth Movements as a Mirror

The mouth speaks long before it utters sound. It tightens, twitches, licks, curls — each microgesture a message from the inner world to the outer one. What we express through our mouths isn't just linguistic — it's deeply psychological.

- **Pressed lips** hold back truth and emotion, waiting for a safe release.
- **Lip licking** reveals what anxiety dares not say aloud.
- **Lip shape**, even when at rest, frames how we are seen — as open books or closed journals.

In conversations where trust, clarity, or connection matter, the mouth often tells you more than the words coming from it. And once you learn to read it — really read it — **you start to hear the silences as clearly as the speech.**

Chapter 2

Body Language Secrets

Female Body Movements and Their Hidden Meanings

Body language is often called the "silent language of the mind." While words express our conscious thoughts, movements reveal subconscious emotions. Female body movements are particularly rich in meaning because they combine social cues, self-image, and emotional states. Understanding these gestures can help you read deeper layers of communication and avoid misinterpretation. When analyzing female body language, context is essential. A single movement rarely tells the whole story; rather, it is the cluster of gestures and the surrounding situation that provide accurate meaning. In this chapter, we will explore three common movements and uncover the hidden messages they may carry.

Hair-playing: Coquettish or Anxious?

Hair-twirling is one of the **most recognizable** female gestures. When a woman wraps a strand of hair around her finger or gently plays with her hair during interaction, it can carry two main interpretations: **attraction** or **anxiety**.

As a sign of flirting, this movement draws attention to the face and neck, which are subtle yet powerful areas of attraction. Combined with *soft eye contact, a slight smile, or leaning closer*, it can indicate interest and openness. In social psychology, hair-twirling in a relaxed context is often viewed as a subconscious way to enhance femininity and invite connection.

As a sign of nervous tension, hair-twirling can act as a **self-soothing mechanism**. When someone feels uneasy or under pressure, repetitive hand movements help release emotional tension. If the action is fast, tense, or paired with *averted eyes*, it is more likely a reflection of discomfort than flirtation.

An additional layer to consider is habit versus intent. Some women develop hair-twirling as a subconscious habit unrelated to mood or social signals. In such cases, look for synchrony between the gesture and emotional context. If the action spikes during specific topics or interactions, it is more likely linked to inner states rather than mere routine.

A further point is the social environment. Hair-twirling during intimate conversations carries a different weight compared to the same action in a formal meeting or public setting. Matching the behavior to the setting helps you determine whether the gesture is personal expression, unconscious habit, or emotional leakage.

Crossed Legs While Standing: A Sign of Self-Protection

Standing with crossed legs is less common than sitting this way, which makes it a more noticeable signal. When a woman stands and crosses her legs, she is literally **reducing the space she occupies**, a movement strongly tied to emotional states.

As a sign of self-protection, crossed legs create a **physical barrier.** This posture can appear in unfamiliar or overwhelming environments where a person subconsciously seeks safety. It is often paired with crossed arms or a lowered chin, forming a defensive cluster of gestures.

As a sign of modesty or shyness, some women naturally adopt this posture when they feel observed. The legs cross to create a sense of containment, signaling a wish to appear smaller or less exposed. Cultural context also matters: *in some societies, this stance is linked with femininity and reserved charm.*

There is also an element of balance and poise. For some, crossing the legs while standing offers physical stability or an aesthetically pleasing posture, especially in social gatherings where presentation matters. Prolonged crossing combined with closed-off gestures, however, leans more toward emotional shielding than comfort.

Another aspect is movement transition. If a woman crosses and uncrosses her legs frequently while standing, it may indicate restlessness or discomfort, while a single, steady crossing often reflects a deliberate emotional state or social presentation. Watching the flow of movement gives more clues than a frozen snapshot.

Hands in Pockets: Cool or Guarded

Hands in pockets is a gesture often associated with casualness, but its meaning changes with posture, environment, and expression. For women, this movement can range from **relaxed confidence** to **emotional withdrawal.**

As a sign of confidence, placing hands in pockets with *open shoulders and steady eye contact* communicates ease and control. It conveys the message "I am comfortable in my space," and is often seen in women who embrace a laid-back yet self-assured style.

As a sign of emotional guarding, hands buried deeply in pockets with *rounded shoulders or averted gaze* can mean withdrawal. The pockets serve as a retreat, symbolically hiding vulnerability and creating distance from others.

An interesting nuance lies in cultural and fashion influence. In some contexts, hands in pockets project modern nonchalance, reflecting confidence shaped by style rather than emotion. Differentiating between this social signal and genuine emotional guarding requires watching for alignment between body and environment.

Body symmetry also plays a role. When hands are loosely in pockets and the upper body remains open, the gesture leans heavily toward ease. Conversely, when both hands are buried and shoulders curve inward, it suggests inner retreat. *The tension or relaxation in surrounding muscles* often reveals the true emotional layer.

Female Movements as a Mirror

In the beginning, we explored how female body movements act as silent messengers, hinting at feelings beneath spoken words. Now, after observing subtle gestures like hair-twirling, crossed legs, and hands tucked into pockets, one truth becomes clear: **body language does not shout; it whispers.**

Unlike the preface, which invites you into the world of interpretation, this closing reflection reminds you of humility. No single gesture defines a person. A woman twirling her hair might be flirting, anxious, or simply lost in thought. Crossed legs may shield vulnerability or just offer balance. Hands in pockets can carry confidence or conceal doubt. **Context, clusters, and compassion turn observation into understanding.**

The essence of reading body movements is not about labeling but about listening without sound. When you pay attention to these whispers, you begin to see what words often fail to reveal: the inner dialogue between emotion and expression. And that is where true connection begins — not in the sentences spoken, but in the movements too subtle to hear yet impossible to ignore.

Female body movements are whispers of the inner world, revealing layers that words often hide. Hair-twirling, crossed legs, and hands in pockets all tell different stories, shaped by context and emotion. The key is not to judge a single gesture but to read clusters, patterns, and subtle shifts. True understanding comes from pairing observation with empathy, allowing movements to become bridges instead of barriers. When you listen to these silent messages, you begin to see the language of presence itself, where every posture and motion speaks of connection, vulnerability, and intent.

Knowing a Person by His Posture

How we stand speaks volumes before we ever say a word. Whether at a networking event, a date, or even just waiting in line, our body reveals cues about our thoughts, emotions, and even long-standing personality traits. Standing postures are among the most honest forms of nonverbal communication because they're largely unconscious. Unlike facial expressions — which we can fake or exaggerate — posture tends to reflect our internal state more authentically. In this article, we explore three common standing cues: upright, military-style posture; forward-leaning stances; and the direction of the toes — and how each may quietly broadcast our values, temperaments, and social dynamics.

Military-Style Standing: Discipline or Dominance?

Imagine someone standing tall, shoulders back, chest out, chin lifted. Their feet are often planted shoulder-width apart, arms relaxed but close to the body, and their overall posture exudes stability and control. This **military-style stance** is often read as a marker of confidence and composure — but it can also signal something more nuanced.

On one hand, this posture is associated with **self-discipline, mental structure, and a preference for order**. People who naturally adopt this posture often value routine, clarity, and personal responsibility. It's common among those with backgrounds in structured environments — military, law enforcement, classical training — but it can also be found in individuals who have cultivated discipline as part of their identity.

On the other hand, this posture can be **read as dominant**, especially when combined with a fixed gaze or minimal facial expression. In hierarchical settings, it can create an unconscious power imbalance: others may feel compelled to defer or follow. The posture creates physical space and symmetry — which, evolutionarily, **communicates strength and leadership**.

But intent matters. Someone standing tall might be trying to **self-regulate**, to feel grounded under pressure. Others may use it to **signal authority**. Context offers clues: in a job interview, this posture may say "I'm composed and capable." In a heated conversation, it might say "I'm standing my ground."

Psychologists often interpret this posture as reflective of **high conscientiousness** and **low neuroticism**. These individuals are seen as organized, reliable, and emotionally steady. But if overused — especially without warmth or flexibility — it may create distance and inhibit vulnerability.

In short, **an upright posture often speaks of internal discipline**, but depending on the setting and demeanor, it may also assert control over the space and people around.

A forward Leaning Means More Prone to Impulsiveness

Now consider someone who's standing but constantly **leaning forward** — perhaps subtly, just a slight tilt at the hips or upper body. This posture gives the impression of **readiness, curiosity, and movement**. It's an active, forward-oriented gesture, and it's often a reliable signal of interest.

Leaning forward during conversation — especially while standing — **usually indicates engagement**. It shows the person is mentally and emotionally "in" the moment, and they want to connect, respond, or act. In romantic or social contexts, it's often interpreted as a sign of attraction or enthusiasm.

But there's a flip side. Chronic forward-leaners, especially those who invade personal space or move without sensing boundaries, may also demonstrate **impulsivity**. They might act before thinking, speak before filtering, or jump into action without calculating risk. **The body, in this case, mirrors the mind: always on the edge of motion.**

This posture is often found in individuals with **high openness and high extraversion.** They're curious, sociable, and drawn to stimulation. But when combined with fidgeting, fast talking, or aggressive eye contact, it may also reflect **restlessness or poor emotional regulation.**

Importantly, posture is context-sensitive. A forward lean during a brainstorming session signals passion. In a tense negotiation, it might be seen as aggressive. In dating, it could either read as eager or invasive, depending on timing and space.

Ultimately, **a forward-leaning posture is an energy cue** — it tells us where a person's mind wants to go: closer, quicker, more. It can be endearing or overwhelming, depending on how well it matches the environment and the interaction.

Where the Toes Point Reveals Who Truly Matters

We often overlook the smallest cues in body language — and the **direction of the feet** is perhaps the most ignored yet revealing signal of social intention.

When standing in a group, we might face someone with our head and shoulders, but our toes often betray who we're *really* invested in. **Toes pointed toward someone signal genuine attention and interest.** Even if the upper body is turned elsewhere, the feet will align with the person we feel most drawn to — emotionally, intellectually, or romantically.

This behavior is rooted in evolutionary biology. Our legs are how we move toward what we desire and away from what we fear. So the position of the feet — particularly when unintentional — reveals **directional intent.** In this way, **our toes act like a social compass**, quietly indicating where our mind and heart are oriented.

In workplace settings, noticing where people's toes point in meetings or casual interactions can reveal **alliances, preferences, or tensions.** Are they turned slightly toward the manager, or angled away from a contentious colleague? In romantic settings, this cue is even more powerful. If someone is speaking to you but their toes are pointed at someone else, their attention may be divided — or directed elsewhere entirely.

The feet can also show discomfort. **Toes angled toward an exit, door, or hallway** suggest a desire to leave — a mental "I'm done here" expressed physically. Even when someone's words are polite, this unconscious posture reveals **disinterest or emotional withdrawal.**

Reading feet direction doesn't require judgment — it simply offers insight. If someone's toes consistently point toward you in a group, chances are you matter more than their words reveal. If they're angled away, especially repeatedly, it may be time to reassess the emotional dynamic.

Feet don't lie — they lead. When it comes to reading intentions, we don't need a loud confession. We just need to look down.

Final Thoughts: The Stillness That Speaks

Standing posture may seem subtle, even boring, compared to facial expressions or hand gestures. But in truth, **our posture is the foundation of our nonverbal story.** It communicates how we view ourselves, how we approach others, and what we expect from the world.

- Military-style standing may reflect a need for internal control — or an attempt to control others.
- Leaning forward might show **a bright eagerness** — or an inability to pause.

- And the feet? They're perhaps the most **honest tell of emotional loyalty.**

As always, posture must be read in **patterns, not moments.** A person may stand tall today because they feel strong, and slouch tomorrow because they're tired — not because their entire personality changed. But over time, the positions we return to most often can say more than we realize.

The way we stand is not just about balance. It's about identity, intention, and how we carry the weight of who we are.

Judging a Person's Thoughts through Gestures

In the following chapters, we explore four powerful gestures that often reveal a person's inner state: the steepled hands that project authority, the crossed arms that create a barrier, the open palms that build instant trust, and the clenched fists that expose deep emotional tension. Each provides not just an explanation of these gestures but also practical understanding of the subtle contexts that give them meaning.

The goal is simple: to teach you how to see beyond words and into the world of unspoken communication. When you can interpret gestures accurately, you not only understand others better but also strengthen your own ability to connect with honesty and respect.

Steepled Hands: Silent Claims of Superiority

When a person forms a steeple with their hands, placing the fingertips together while keeping the palms apart, they are often communicating more than words ever could. This gesture is a subtle yet powerful expression of confidence and authority. In many cases, it signals a belief in one's own knowledge or position within a conversation. The steepled hands are often observed in individuals who feel in control of a situation, whether in a professional meeting, a negotiation, or even in casual conversation.

The gesture creates a frame of calm assertiveness. The fingers point upwards like a structure of strength, giving the impression that the person is weighing ideas carefully and from a position of intellectual or emotional dominance. Many leaders and executives unconsciously use this gesture when they want to project control. When someone maintains this posture while listening, it often indicates they believe they are more knowledgeable than the speaker. If used during speaking, it tends to emphasize their certainty about their statements.

However, context matters greatly. In a supportive environment, steepled hands can suggest a mentor-like confidence, signaling a desire to share wisdom. In a more confrontational setting, the same gesture can reveal a sense of superiority or silent challenge. Observing when and how this gesture appears gives valuable insight into the person's internal state, whether they are trying to assert dominance, reassure themselves, or guide the conversation.

Crossed Arms: The Shield of Deception

Crossed arms are among the most recognized nonverbal gestures, often interpreted as defensiveness or resistance. While that interpretation holds some truth, the deeper meaning behind crossed arms lies in the psychological instinct to protect oneself. By folding the arms across the chest, a person subconsciously creates a barrier between themselves and others. This gesture can signal discomfort, insecurity, or the need to hide true intentions.

In conversations where trust is uncertain, crossed arms can act as a silent shield. A person may be trying to mask vulnerability or avoid revealing their thoughts. In some cases, it reflects an unwillingness to accept what is being said. In negotiation settings, it often appears when one party feels pressured or skeptical about the terms being presented.

Crossed arms are also linked to deception because they can coincide with a person's attempt to conceal inner conflict. When someone is lying or withholding information, the body instinctively seeks a protective posture. Crossing the arms helps them create a psychological wall, as though keeping their secrets from leaking out.

Yet, not every instance of crossed arms means dishonesty. It may also signal self-comfort, especially in situations where the person feels cold or overwhelmed. The key is to observe accompanying signals: tense shoulders, avoidance of eye contact, or subtle movements of the lips can confirm whether the gesture is defensive or deceptive. Understanding this gesture requires paying attention to the surrounding emotional climate and the person's overall body language.

Open Palms: Building Instant Trust

The gesture of open palms has been recognized for centuries as a universal signal of honesty and openness. When someone exposes the inner side of their hands during conversation, they are often unconsciously demonstrating a lack of threat. This gesture dates back to primal human instincts; showing the palms meant showing one had no weapon, thus signaling safety and trust.

In modern communication, open palms still carry this deep psychological weight. A person who uses open palm gestures while speaking tends to come across as transparent and genuine. It conveys a willingness to share thoughts and emotions without hidden motives. Leaders who wish to inspire confidence often adopt this gesture naturally. It softens their message, making their words more approachable and believable.

The position of the palms adds nuance to the message. Palms facing upward suggest offering and invitation, creating a sense of inclusion. Palms facing outward can signal sincerity and a desire for peace, often seen when someone is trying to calm a tense situation. Even subtle flashes of open palms during conversation can shift the emotional tone and increase trust between parties.

However, false use of the gesture can also occur. Some individuals consciously exaggerate open palm movements to manipulate trust. In these cases, the rest of the body may betray the act through stiffness, lack of genuine facial expressions, or inconsistent eye contact. True openness is usually accompanied by relaxed shoulders and congruent emotional cues. Recognizing these small details helps distinguish between authentic and staged gestures.

To illustrate the subtle power of choice and control in social interactions — often mirrored in body language and gestures — consider these everyday examples:

Example 1: When guests arrive at your home, if you ask, "Would you like something to drink?" most will politely decline, even if they are thirsty. However, if you instead ask, "Would you like coffee or water?" most will choose one option, even if moments before they said no.

The difference lies in how you position the question: the second approach places people in a decision-making role and subtly guides them within the range of options you control.

Example 2: Imagine you are walking down the street and someone hands you a camera, asking, "Can you take a picture for me?" Without hesitation, you likely accept and help. This quick, automatic response shows how simple social gestures and framed choices influence behavior beyond conscious thought.

These examples underscore how our gestures and questions influence not only what we communicate but how others respond—building trust, controlling interactions, or creating psychological barriers. Being aware of this can enhance your ability to read and influence social dynamics effectively.

Clenched Fists: A Signal of Deep Resentment

Few gestures carry as much raw emotional energy as clenched fists. When the fingers curl tightly into the palm and the knuckles tense, the body is preparing for a fight, whether physical or psychological. This gesture reflects suppressed aggression or intense emotional struggle. It is often seen in moments of deep frustration, anger, or resentment that the person is trying to control.

Clenched fists can manifest subtly, such as a hand tightening momentarily during conversation. This micro-gesture often signals that a person is emotionally triggered but attempting to maintain composure. In more obvious cases, both hands may form fists while the arms stiffen, creating a clear display of inner conflict. In either form, the gesture reveals the presence of powerful emotions hidden beneath the surface.

In social interactions, clenched fists can indicate disagreement that the person is reluctant to voice. It can also be a sign of resistance to authority or a signal that boundaries are being tested. In relationships, noticing this gesture may help identify unresolved tension or unspoken resentment before it escalates.

Not all clenched fists are born of anger. In some cases, they signal determination or intense focus. Athletes often clench their fists before a challenging performance, channeling energy into strength. The surrounding context, facial expressions, and tone of voice help distinguish whether the gesture is rooted in aggression or resolve.

Hand Gesture as a Mirror

Understanding these gestures is vital because they offer a rare window into emotions people often try to hide. Unlike words, which can be chosen carefully, these gestures are raw reflections of the body's internal state. They serve as warning signs, calls to pay attention to the emotional undercurrents of interactions. When you learn to recognize these signals, you gain an invaluable tool to understand not just what people say, but what they truly feel and think.

Beyond Gestures: The Power of Context and Framing

While body language offers a treasure trove of insights, it is important to remember that gestures do not exist in isolation. Their meaning often depends heavily on the context, cultural background, and the interplay with verbal communication. For instance, crossed arms might signal defensiveness in one culture but simply comfort in another. Similarly, a gesture that conveys confidence in a business meeting may be perceived as arrogance in a more informal setting.

Moreover, the way we frame our questions and interactions can subtly influence not only others' responses but also the gestures they use. Framing a question as a choice rather than an open-ended invitation can make someone more likely to engage positively, as shown in the examples above. This reflects a deeper psychological principle: people naturally respond better when they feel a sense of control, even within limits set by others.

Mastering the ability to observe and interpret these combined cues — gestures, context, verbal framing — gives you a powerful edge in personal and professional communication. It allows you to navigate conversations with empathy, detect underlying tensions early, and build trust more effectively.

Judging a Person's Thoughts by Their Sitting Posture

The way a person sits can reveal a wealth of information about their thoughts, feelings, and intentions. Body language experts often emphasize that nonverbal cues are crucial in understanding others, sometimes even more than the words they speak. Among the various body language signals, **sitting posture stands out as a significant indicator of confidence, openness, and psychological state.** This chapter explores three key sitting postures—open posture, leg-crossing, and leaning in—and what they reveal about a person's mindset.

Open posture while sitting: a sign of confidence

When a person adopts an open posture while sitting, it often communicates **confidence and self-assurance.** Open posture typically involves *sitting upright with arms and legs uncrossed, shoulders relaxed, and the chest slightly forward.* This stance suggests the person feels comfortable and **in control of the situation.**

An open posture signals that the individual is **approachable** and **receptive.** Without barriers like crossed arms or legs, the body language conveys **a willingness to engage and listen.** Such a posture can also indicate emotional openness and honesty. People who sit openly tend to be less guarded and more **transparent** in their interactions.

Moreover, open sitting postures are linked to higher levels of confidence. Research in psychology shows that adopting expansive body language can **increase feelings of self-esteem and reduce stress.** This phenomenon, sometimes called "*power posing,*" helps people project strength and positivity, even in challenging situations.

In social or professional settings, noticing someone's open posture can help you identify those who are self-assured and ready to participate actively. They may be more willing to share their ideas, accept feedback, and collaborate effectively. Open posture also facilitates **better breathing and circulation,** contributing to overall alertness and mental clarity.

On the other hand, a closed posture, such as *slouching or curling up*, can indicate **discomfort, insecurity, or a desire to withdraw.** It is important to observe posture in the context of other nonverbal cues and situational factors, but open sitting generally serves as a reliable indicator of confidence.

Leg-crossing: confidence or psychological defense?

Crossing one's legs while sitting is a common gesture that can convey different messages depending on the **context** and **individual personality**. For some, leg-crossing is a **habitual, comfortable** position that has little to do with emotions. For others, it may be a subtle form of **psychological defense or assertion of dominance.**

When someone crosses their legs with ease and a relaxed demeanor, it often signals **confidence**. This posture can reflect a person's comfort in their environment and their self-possession. It creates a sense of controlled poise and can make the individual appear more composed and elegant.

However, leg-crossing can also serve as a **protective barrier.** *Crossing the legs tightly or with the foot pointed away from others* may suggest a subconscious attempt to create distance or shield oneself from emotional exposure. In such cases, it might indicate **discomfort, defensiveness,** or **hesitation**.

Body language experts caution against reading leg-crossing in isolation. The meaning depends heavily on other signs such as facial expression, arm positioning, and the nature of the interaction. For example, crossing legs while leaning away from a speaker might signal **reluctance** or **resistance**, whereas crossing legs while leaning forward could still reflect **engagement**.

It is also important to consider cultural differences. In some cultures, certain leg-crossing postures may have specific social connotations. Observing how leg-crossing aligns with verbal communication and situational context is crucial for accurate interpretation.

In **professional settings**, leg-crossing combined with an upright posture and eye contact often conveys **authority** and **self-assurance**. In more **casual environments**, it might simply be a **comfortable** resting position. Understanding these nuances allows one to better judge a person's internal state.

Leaning in: engaged or eager to please?

Leaning in while sitting is a powerful nonverbal cue that reveals the person's level of interest and engagement. When someone *leans forward,* they physically **close the distance** between themselves and the speaker or object of attention, signaling **attentiveness** and **involvement**.

Leaning in often indicates that the individual is **actively listening, eager to understand**, or **emotionally invested in the conversation.** It creates an impression of sincerity and genuine interest, which can build trust and rapport.

However, leaning in can sometimes be interpreted as **eagerness to please**, especially if accompanied by submissive gestures like *nodding excessively, avoiding eye contact, or smiling nervously*. In such cases, the posture may reflect **a desire to gain approval** rather than authentic engagement.

Discerning between genuine involvement and eagerness to please requires careful observation of the overall body language and context. For example, if the person *leans in but frequently glances away or shows signs of anxiety,* it may indicate **underlying insecurity or pressure to conform.**

Conversely, a confident person who leans in usually maintains *steady eye contact, relaxed facial expressions,* and *open gestures*. This posture can **enhance communication** by encouraging openness and creating a collaborative atmosphere.

Leaning in is also a useful tactic in **negotiation and persuasion**, as it **reduces psychological distance** and **fosters connection**. People tend to respond positively to those who demonstrate active participation through forward posture.

In summary, leaning in is a valuable indicator of a person's mindset, but it must be assessed alongside other behavioral signals to accurately understand their true thoughts and feelings.

Sitting Posture as a Mirror

Sitting posture offers a silent window into the human mind. Every subtle adjustment of the body reflects underlying emotions, attitudes, and levels of confidence. An *open posture* often signals **comfort, strength,** and **a willingness to engage,** while *leg-crossing* can **fluctuate between** calm self-assurance **and** a subtle need for protection. **Leaning in** reflects **a desire to connect,** though it may also expose an eagerness to gain approval when combined with other submissive gestures.

Interpreting these cues requires more than observing a single movement. True understanding comes from viewing posture as part of a broader behavioral pattern, where **context, environment, and accompanying signals play critical roles.** When read carefully, these nonverbal messages can uncover layers of thought and intention that words alone cannot convey.

Mastering the art of reading sitting postures not only deepens interpersonal awareness but also strengthens communication skills. It allows you to respond with greater empathy, recognize hidden emotions, and adapt your approach in social and professional settings. Ultimately, by observing how people position themselves when seated, you gain a powerful tool for judging thoughts and building more authentic, meaningful connections.

The Psychology of Touch

Touch is one of the most profound and primal forms of human communication. Long before words were spoken, **touch served as a way to convey safety, affection, dominance, and even warnings.** Unlike verbal language, which can be masked or manipulated, touch often reflects **unconscious feelings** and **hidden intentions.**

Understanding the subtle variations in human touch provides valuable insights into **relationships, power dynamics,** and **emotional states.** This chapter explores the nuances of touch through three common scenarios, each revealing the complex psychology behind physical contact.

A Light Tap on the Shoulder: Encouragement or Subtle Control?

A gentle tap on the shoulder may seem like an insignificant gesture, yet it carries layers of meaning. **In social and**

professional settings, a light tap is often used to **draw attention or offer reassurance**. When a teacher taps a student's shoulder, it may signal **support or acknowledgment**. Similarly, in a workplace, a manager's gentle tap might be intended as a subtle form of encouragement, indicating trust and inclusion. In these contexts, the tap serves as a bridge between authority and empathy.

However, the same gesture can also convey **subtle control**. A person tapping another on the shoulder to **redirect their focus or interrupt a conversation** is exercising a small but clear assertion of dominance. The individual receiving the tap must shift their attention, creating a momentary imbalance of power. This is especially evident when the tap is combined with firm eye contact or a directive tone of voice.

Cultural background plays a significant role in how this gesture is interpreted. **In more tactile cultures**, a shoulder tap may be viewed as a natural extension of conversation, carrying **warmth** and **friendliness. In cultures where personal space is more strictly observed**, it can feel **intrusive**, making the recipient **unconsciously defensive.** The context, relationship between the individuals, and accompanying body language all contribute to decoding the true intention.

To differentiate between encouragement and control, it is essential to observe the overall energy of the interaction. An *encouraging tap* is usually **brief, light**, and followed by an *open facial expression or verbal affirmation*. A *controlling tap* tends to linger slightly *longer* or is accompanied by a *directive movement,* such as guiding the person in a particular direction. Recognizing this distinction can reveal the subtle power dynamics at play in everyday interactions.

Strength of Handshake Reveals Intention of Cooperation

The handshake remains one of the most universally recognized forms of greeting, yet its psychological weight extends far beyond a simple hello. The firmness of a handshake often communicates unspoken messages about **confidence, dominance**, or even **insecurity**. A *balanced handshake* — firm but not crushing — typically reflects **self-assurance** and **mutual respect**. It creates a sense of equality between the two parties and establishes a foundation for open communication.

A handshake that is **too forceful**, on the other hand, often signals a desire to **assert dominance** or **control**. In professional settings, individuals who use excessive pressure may be attempting to establish authority early in the interaction. While some perceive a strong handshake as a sign of confidence, when the pressure crosses into discomfort, it becomes a power move rather than a gesture of connection. Conversely, a *limp handshake* can suggest **nervousness, lack of confidence,** or **disinterest.** In some cases, it is also used deliberately as a passive-aggressive tactic, signaling detachment or **resistance to connection.**

Beyond pressure, other subtle elements influence the psychological message of a handshake. The *duration of the shake,* the *amount of eye contact maintained,* and even *the positioning of the hands* can indicate status and intent. For example, when one person turns their hand to face upward, allowing the other to cover it, it can signal submission or a desire to please. When the hand is rotated downward or remains firmly on top, it conveys **dominance** and **control** over the exchange.

Cultural norms once again shape interpretation. In **Western business environments,** a *firm handshake* is almost mandatory and **equated with professionalism. In other cultures,** a *softer handshake* may be **a sign of respect** rather than weakness. Understanding these nuances helps in accurately reading intentions rather than misjudging them based on personal cultural standards.

To accurately interpret a handshake, one must consider context, consistency, and accompanying non-verbal cues. Is the firm grip paired with a genuine smile and relaxed posture, or is it combined with a piercing gaze and stiff demeanor? **Such details can distinguish between confidence, aggression, and insecurity, turning a simple greeting into a window into someone's true character.**

Unconscious Touching: Intimacy or Boundary Violation?

Unconscious touching is perhaps one of the most revealing forms of physical communication because it bypasses deliberate control. **When someone absentmindedly places a hand on another's arm during conversation, it can signify warmth, connection, and a desire for closeness.** This kind of touch often strengthens emotional bonds and enhances trust between individuals. In romantic contexts, unconscious touch frequently signals attraction or affection that the person may not even be fully aware of expressing.

However, **unconscious touching is not always perceived positively.** When such contact **crosses personal boundaries**, it can evoke **discomfort** or even **alarm.** For instance, if a colleague repeatedly touches another person's arm or shoulder without realizing it, the recipient may interpret it as a breach of professional boundaries. The reaction to this kind of touch is highly dependent on the **relationship** between the individuals and the **environment** in which it occurs. What feels **intimate** and **comforting** in a **close friendship** may feel **invasive** in a **formal or unfamiliar setting.**

Another factor to consider is the *location of the touch*. Light contact on the arm or hand often conveys friendliness and emotional support, whereas touching more private areas such as the *lower back* or *waist* can suggest **dominance** or

inappropriate familiarity. The intensity and duration of the touch further shape its interpretation. **Brief, light contact** may go **unnoticed**, while **prolonged or repetitive touching** often triggers a **stronger emotional response.**

Unconscious touching can also reveal inner emotional states. People experiencing anxiety may touch others more frequently as a way to seek reassurance. Conversely, those feeling powerful or in control may use touch to subtly reinforce their status. Observing patterns over time — who the person touches, when, and how — offers deep insight into their comfort levels, intentions, and emotional dynamics.

To determine whether unconscious touch reflects intimacy or a boundary violation, one must consider the recipient's reaction. If the person being touched instinctively leans in, maintains open body language, or mirrors the gesture, the touch is likely interpreted as positive. If they pull away, stiffen, or avoid eye contact, it may indicate discomfort or a perceived breach of personal space. Learning to recognize these responses allows for a more accurate reading of the underlying emotional and relational context.

Touch as a Mirror

Touch, in its many forms, is a powerful yet often overlooked language. *A light tap on the shoulder* can **uplift** or **control.** A *handshake* can **equalize** or **dominate.** *Unconscious touch* can **connect hearts** or **cross boundaries.** Each subtle variation offers clues to the unspoken emotions and intentions behind human interaction. By paying close attention to these nuances, one can unlock a deeper understanding of others and navigate social and professional relationships with greater insight and empathy.

Chapter 3

Voice & Speech Secrets

What a Person's Voice Revealsabout Their Personality

The human voice is far more than a tool for conveying words; it is an instrument of emotional and psychological expression. **Subtle variations** in tone, pitch, and rhythm can reveal layers of a person's personality that are often hidden beneath carefully chosen language. While body language and facial expressions are widely studied, vocal cues provide an equally rich source of information about **inner states, confidence levels**, and **emotional balance.** Understanding these vocal patterns allows us to read between the lines of conversation and uncover truths about the speaker's character and intentions.

Rising Tone: Seeking Approval or Insecure?

A rising tone at the end of sentences is a common vocal pattern that carries a complex range of meanings. On the surface, it often sounds like a question, even when the statement is not interrogative. This upward inflection can suggest a desire for validation, signaling that the speaker is seeking approval or confirmation from their audience. In social dynamics, people who use a rising tone frequently may be expressing a subconscious need for reassurance, indicating a personality that leans toward agreeableness or social sensitivity.

However, a **rising tone** can also reflect **underlying insecurity.** When someone consistently ends statements with an upward inflection, it can give the impression that they are unsure of their own words or lack confidence in their perspective. In professional environments, this vocal pattern is sometimes interpreted as a sign of hesitation or lack of authority, even if the speaker possesses strong knowledge or expertise. For this reason, individuals in **leadership roles** are often trained to **maintain a neutral or downward tone** to convey **confidence and decisiveness.**

Cultural and contextual factors play a significant role in how a rising tone is perceived. In some regions, such as parts of Australia and California, upward inflection at the end of sentences has become a normalized speech pattern and does not necessarily indicate insecurity. In other settings, especially in formal communication, the same tone can undermine the perceived strength of the message. Observers must carefully separate cultural norms from psychological signals to avoid misinterpretation.

To determine whether a rising tone reflects a simple conversational style, a need for approval, or deeper insecurity, one must consider the speaker's body language, consistency of tone, and situational context. When paired with **nervous gestures, avoiding eye contact, or self-effacing language,** the rising tone is more likely to **signal insecurity.** When combined with warmth, open posture, and confident content, it can simply reflect a desire to connect and engage. Understanding this nuance allows us to read the voice as a subtle yet revealing indicator of personality.

Flat Tone: Calm Demeanor or Emotional Detachment?

A flat tone, characterized by **little variation in pitch**, can convey multiple layers of meaning. At its best, it reflects a **calm, composed demeanor.** People with naturally even vocal patterns often exude steadiness, rationality, and control over their emotions. In high-pressure situations, a flat tone can project authority and reliability, making others feel secure in the speaker's presence. For this reason, many professionals in leadership, law enforcement, or negotiation roles cultivate a more neutral tone to maintain composure and clarity.

Yet a flat tone can also suggest emotional detachment or lack of engagement. **When a voice lacks warmth or variation, it can create distance between the speaker and listener, making the interaction feel impersonal or cold.** In interpersonal relationships, a consistently monotone voice may hint at emotional suppression or difficulty expressing feelings. Some individuals adopt this vocal style as a defense mechanism, using neutrality to protect themselves from vulnerability.

Context is critical in interpreting a flat tone. In professional or crisis scenarios, it may be a deliberate choice to maintain stability and avoid escalation. In personal conversations, especially those involving emotional topics, **a lack of vocal inflection may signal discomfort or a reluctance to connect on a deeper level.** Observing facial expressions, pacing, and word choice alongside the tone can help clarify whether the neutrality reflects strength and calm or emotional withdrawal.

A flat tone can also be influenced by cultural factors. In some cultures, maintaining a composed voice is seen as a sign of respect and maturity. **In others, expressive intonation is valued as a sign of honesty and emotional openness.** When assessing personality through vocal cues, it is essential to account for these differences and avoid projecting one's own cultural expectations onto another's speech patterns.

To distinguish between calm composure and emotional detachment, listen for subtle shifts within the flat tone. Even in a neutral delivery, small variations in pacing or slight softening on key words can reveal underlying warmth. Conversely, a completely uniform tone with minimal emphasis or inflection often points to emotional distance or disengagement. Mastering the ability to decode these subtleties can provide profound insights into both the speaker's personality and their current emotional state.

Variable Tones Means Emotion Fluctuating

At the opposite end of the spectrum lies dramatic intonation, marked by significant rises and falls in pitch and rhythm. **A voice rich in variation** often conveys emotional expressiveness and passion. People with naturally dramatic intonation tend to be perceived as charismatic, engaging, and full of vitality. Their voices capture attention and draw listeners into the conversation, **making them powerful** communicators in both personal and public settings. This vocal style often reflects a personality that is **comfortable with emotional transparency and enjoys connection through shared feeling.**

But dramatic vocal delivery can also be used strategically.
One memorable example comes from a real-world negotiation between a clever entrepreneur and a property seller. The entrepreneur wanted to acquire a commercial property originally priced at $2.5 million. He suspected the market would drop soon and aimed to buy at $2.2 million or less. Instead of starting with a reasonable offer, he began dramatically low, saying: "I love the location, but I can only offer $2 million." The seller immediately declined.

Three days later, the entrepreneur called again — with a shift in both tone and message. "I managed to convince my partner to raise our offer," he said, this time with more gravity and sincerity in his voice. "We can go up to $2.1 million." The seller didn't accept but began to hesitate.

Finally, the entrepreneur made one last call: "I've done everything I can. We're at $2.2 million. That's the absolute limit. If it's reasonable to you, let's talk." After weeks without better offers, the seller agreed. What worked wasn't just the numbers — it was the calculated use of dramatic pacing, emotional delivery, and shifts in vocal tone to create pressure, establish contrast, and emotionally anchor each new offer. This is known in psychology as the "door in the face" technique: start high or low to invite rejection, then follow up with something more reasonable that feels like a concession.

This case highlights how **intonation**, especially when paired with timing and narrative, can manipulate perceptions of sincerity, urgency, or goodwill. The spoken voice becomes a **performance**, shaping emotional reality even more than facts. Of course, not all dramatic intonation is manipulative. When it matches the content and emotional tone of the conversation, it reflects authenticity and enthusiasm. But when the delivery feels disconnected from the subject matter or is exaggerated for effect, it may hint at instability or an attempt to steer perception.

Cultural influence again shapes interpretation. In some cultures, animated speech is a sign of warmth and sincerity, while in others, restraint is valued as a marker of self-control.

What appears dramatic to one listener may feel completely natural to another. This underscores the importance of reading vocal patterns in relation to the speaker's broader cultural and personal context rather than in isolation.

To evaluate dramatic intonation accurately, observe how it affects the interaction. Does the variation draw people in, foster connection, and align with the message, or does it create discomfort and distract from the content? Balanced expressiveness often indicates emotional intelligence and vibrant personality, while erratic or exaggerated patterns may point to inner turbulence or a need for validation through performance.

Voice as a Mirror

The human voice is a mirror of the inner self. **A rising tone** can reveal a search for approval or hint at hidden insecurity. **A flat tone** may project calm strength or mask emotional distance. **Dramatic intonation** can bring life and warmth to communication or expose instability beneath the surface.
But as the story of the property negotiation shows, **intonation is also a tool**—a way to shape perception, negotiate influence, and steer emotion. When we learn to listen not just to what is said but how it's said, we uncover the silent signals of personality and intent.

By learning to listen beyond words and decode these subtle vocal cues, we gain access to a deeper understanding of personality and emotional truth. Mastering the art of interpreting voices not only enhances communication but also opens a window into the intricate landscape of human character.

What a Person's Pitch Is Really Saying

The human voice is one of the most powerful tools for communication, yet its true messages often lie beyond the words spoken. Among the many elements of vocal expression, pitch stands out as a subtle but profound indicator of personality, emotion, and intention. Long before we consciously analyze what someone says, we react instinctively to how they say it. *A lower tone* can create an impression of **authority and strength**, while *a higher one* might suggest **openness, vulnerability, or emotional intensity.** These vocal cues operate at a level deeper than language, influencing the way we perceive others in both personal and professional settings.

This chapter explores **the hidden meanings behind vocal pitch**, uncovering the unspoken signals that shape our interactions every day. From the commanding resonance of a deep voice to the lively expressiveness of higher tones, pitch offers a window into the inner world of the speaker. Understanding these subtle shifts allows us to read beyond words and grasp the emotional truths people often try to conceal. By learning to interpret vocal pitch, we not only gain insight into others but also discover how our own voices influence the way the world perceives us.

Lower Pitch: The Voice of Natural Leader

When you hear a person speak with a *lower pitch*, it often carries a weight that instantly **captures attention**. A *deep voice* has long been associated with **leadership, strength,** and **confidence**. This association is not accidental. Across cultures and generations, a lower pitch has been linked to individuals who are perceived as authoritative. There is a primal aspect to this reaction. In nature, lower frequencies often signify size and dominance, from the growl of a predator to the resonance of a large drum. Human perception still carries this instinctive bias.

People with naturally *lower voices* often find that others **listen to them more attentively**. In professional environments, a calm and deep tone can project competence and command **respect**. Politicians, leaders, and executives who maintain a steady, lower pitch often find their words carrying more weight. However, it is not only the natural pitch but also how the person uses it. **A controlled, deliberate voice in the lower range communicates not only authority but also composure and confidence.**

That said, the voice of natural authority is not just about sounding commanding. It also conveys **security** and **reassurance.** When a leader speaks with a lower pitch, it gives the impression of someone who can handle pressure and guide others through challenges. This quality explains why people often describe such voices as grounding or calming. The ability to project strength **without aggression** creates a balance that draws others in rather than pushing them away.

It is important to recognize that a *lower pitch* **does not always equal dominance.** Some individuals adopt a lower pitch consciously to project authority, even when it is not their natural tone. While this can be effective to some degree, the voice may lose authenticity if forced. Listeners are highly sensitive to subtle changes in tone and can sense when someone is straining to sound different from their natural state. **True vocal authority comes not only from pitch but also from alignment between voice, emotion, and intention.**

Interestingly, studies show that *lower-pitched* voices in *men* are often perceived as **more attractive** and **trustworthy,** while for *women,* a moderate to slightly *lower pitch* tends to be associated with **maturity** and **confidence.** This perception highlights how much vocal pitch can shape first impressions and interpersonal dynamics. When evaluating someone's voice, the key is to notice whether the lower pitch is consistent and natural or used selectively to influence others.

Higher Pitch: Submissiveness or Just Expressiveness?

A *higher-pitched voice* often evokes a different set of associations. In many cultures, a high pitch has been linked to **submissiveness, nervousness**, or **lack of authority.** People who speak in a consistently high tone may be perceived as less dominant, and in professional settings, this can sometimes work against them. However, equating high pitch solely with weakness is an oversimplification. The reality is far more nuanced.

High pitch can also be a sign of **expressiveness** and **emotional intensity.** When people are *excited, passionate,* or *deeply engaged in a conversation,* their pitch naturally rises. **This is a universal human trait.** A higher pitch can convey enthusiasm, warmth, and openness. It often draws people in emotionally, making the speaker appear approachable and energetic. In this way, what some interpret as a lack of authority can also be understood as **a sign of vitality and human connection.**

There is also a **gendered perception of pitch.** *Women typically have higher-pitched voices* due to physiological differences, but this does not automatically make their voices submissive.

In fact, many female leaders use a higher range effectively to convey clarity and emotional resonance. The challenge lies in balancing pitch with control. A voice that fluctuates wildly in the high range, especially under stress, may indeed communicate anxiety or lack of confidence. Conversely, a controlled, expressive high pitch can demonstrate engagement and emotional intelligence.

Cultural context also shapes how high pitch is interpreted. In some societies, a *softer, higher tone* is associated with **politeness** and **respect**, especially in hierarchical relationships. What might seem submissive in one culture could be seen as socially intelligent in another. Therefore, when reading a person's pitch, it is critical to consider the surrounding social and cultural framework rather than applying a universal interpretation.

One of the most telling aspects of a higher pitch is whether it is **situational** or **habitual**. If a person's pitch rises only during moments of excitement or emotional expression, it likely reflects natural enthusiasm. However, if the pitch remains high across all interactions, especially during moments requiring calm authority, it might suggest insecurity or an attempt to please others. The subtle variations in when and how pitch rises offer deeper insights into a person's emotional state and personality.

Deeper Voices Equals to Control Situation More Easily

The idea that deeper voices command more respect is one of the most persistent beliefs in human communication. From historical figures to modern leaders, society often celebrates the voice that resonates in a lower range as a marker of strength and credibility. But why does this perception exist, and is it always accurate?

From an evolutionary perspective, a deeper voice signals physical maturity and stability. In many species, vocal depth correlates with body size and strength. Humans have retained this instinctive association. When someone speaks with a deep voice, it subconsciously activates a sense of presence and influence. This explains why deeper voices are often preferred in roles requiring leadership, persuasion, or authority, such as politics, law, and broadcasting.

However, respect earned through a deeper voice is not guaranteed. A deep tone without emotional warmth can come across as intimidating or detached. True respect is a combination of how the voice is used and the character it reflects. A leader who combines a deep voice with empathy and clarity can command respect naturally, while someone who uses a deep pitch to dominate without connection may only inspire fear or resistance.

There is also a question of authenticity. Not everyone with a deep voice is automatically respected, and not everyone with a higher voice struggles to earn respect. What matters is vocal congruence: the alignment of pitch, tone, and message. **When a person's voice matches their intentions and emotions, it resonates as genuine, regardless of pitch.** This is why some individuals with moderate or even higher-pitched voices still command immense respect — they project authenticity and confidence through consistent vocal control.

It is also worth noting that the link between deeper voices and respect is shifting in modern communication. As workplaces emphasize collaboration and emotional intelligence, respect is less tied to dominance and more to connection. While a deep voice can still serve as an advantage, the ability to modulate pitch and adapt to different contexts may carry equal weight. A leader who can shift between a deep authoritative tone and a lighter, more approachable pitch demonstrates versatility, earning respect through adaptability rather than sheer vocal depth.

Ultimately, **the question is** not whether deeper voices always command more respect, but **how pitch interacts with authenticity, intention, and cultural expectations**. A voice, whether deep or high, becomes powerful when it reflects the speaker's true self and communicates confidence without pretense. Understanding this balance allows us to look beyond the surface of pitch and into the deeper layers of personality and communication style.

What a Person's Speaking Speed Says About Him

Speaking speed is more than a habit; it is a reflection of thought and emotion. Before words are understood, the pace of speech shapes how we perceive the speaker. *Rapid speech* can hint at **guilt** or **anxiety**, while *delayed responses* may reveal **hesitation** or mental distance. When the pace shifts unpredictably, it often signals emotional turbulence or intentional control. This chapter explores how tempo uncovers hidden truths behind conversations. By learning to read these subtle vocal rhythms, we gain deeper insight into character and intention, hearing not just what is said but what lies beneath the words.

Speed up Speech: Voiceprint Evidence of Guilt

When someone *speaks rapidly*, words often tumble out in a way that feels **uncontrolled** or **anxious.** Fast speech has long been associated with heightened emotional states, and one of the most common interpretations is that it signals guilt. The reasoning is simple: **when people are hiding something or feel trapped, their minds race ahead of their mouths, trying to cover gaps and avoid exposure.** This mental rush translates into vocal speed, creating what many consider to be the vocal fingerprints of guilt.

However, rapid speech does not always mean a person is being dishonest. It can also reflect nervousness, excitement, or an attempt to fill silence. The key lies in context and consistency. For example, *someone accused of wrongdoing* who suddenly accelerates their speech while offering explanations may indeed be revealing an **internal struggle** to control information. In contrast, a *naturally fast talker* who maintains the same speed in casual and serious conversations is likely expressing **personality** rather than guilt.

Rapid speech can also be a defense mechanism. **People under pressure may instinctively try to control the flow of conversation, overwhelming the listener with words to leave less room for scrutiny.** This pattern is particularly noticeable in situations where truth is being tested, such as *interviews,* *interrogations,* or *tense negotiations.* The rush of words serves both as a shield and as a way to regain control of the narrative.

From a psychological perspective, guilt often creates physiological arousal — *faster heartbeat, increased adrenaline,* and *heightened alertness.* These physical responses can manifest in vocal patterns, including a quicker tempo. Listeners may not consciously analyze the speech speed, but they sense the underlying tension. This instinctive reaction explains why rapid speech often makes others suspicious even when no concrete evidence is present.

At the same time, **cultural and personality factors play a role.** In some cultures, a lively, fast-paced speaking style is the norm and does not carry negative implications. Extroverted individuals may naturally process thoughts quickly and express them in rapid succession without any emotional burden. Therefore, it is crucial to look for changes rather than absolute speed. **If a typically calm speaker suddenly accelerates their words in a sensitive moment, that shift is more revealing than the speed itself.**

Ultimately, rapid speech is less about guilt as a universal truth and more about incongruence between words and emotional state. When the pace of speech does not match the situation or the speaker's usual rhythm, it raises questions. The voice becomes a window into the inner turmoil, whether it is guilt, fear, or a desperate need to be believed.

Delayed Responses: A Sign of Mental Absence

On the opposite end of the spectrum, delayed responses often communicate something equally telling. *A pause before speaking* can indicate **careful thought,** but when delays are *consistent or exaggerated,* they may reveal **a lack of presence or engagement.** In conversations, speech is not just about words but also about timing. When timing feels off, it disrupts the flow and draws attention to the speaker's internal state.

A delayed response can signal that the mind is elsewhere. Perhaps the person is **distracted, uninterested, or emotionally detached from the situation.** This mental absence becomes evident when answers come too slowly to match the natural rhythm of dialogue. Listeners may interpret this as disconnection or even as an attempt to fabricate answers. The human brain is attuned to conversational patterns, so deviations from the expected tempo are often read as signs of something hidden or missing.

At times, delayed speech is a strategy rather than a symptom. **Skilled negotiators** or **leaders** may *pause intentionally* to create weight behind their words or to control the pace of interaction. This deliberate delay is usually accompanied by steady body language and a sense of purpose. In contrast, a delay caused by mental absence lacks focus and creates discomfort rather than authority.

Psychologically, delayed responses can stem from several sources. Anxiety may cause a person to overthink every word, resulting in unnatural pauses. Fatigue or emotional overload can slow cognitive processing, making speech lag behind thought. In some cases, the delay reflects an internal conflict: **the mind is working through competing truths or crafting a version of reality that fits the moment.** These subtle distinctions are where speaking speed becomes an indicator of deeper emotional and mental states.

Social context again plays a crucial role. In cultures that value careful speech and reflection, a measured pace may be seen as wisdom rather than absence. However, when the delay exceeds cultural norms or lacks coherence with the situation, it still stands out as a red flag. For example, when someone is asked a direct question and takes unusually long to answer, the pause often feels loaded, as if something unsaid lingers in the silence.

Delayed responses can also reveal power dynamics. In conversations where one person holds emotional or social dominance, the other may respond more slowly out of hesitation or fear of saying the wrong thing. This hesitation is not mental absence in the sense of disengagement but rather a sign of suppressed expression. In these cases, the delay becomes a window into a deeper imbalance between the individuals.

Ultimately, the significance of delayed responses lies in whether the timing aligns with genuine reflection or signals disconnection. When speech lags without purpose or emotional resonance, it often points to a mind that is not fully present in the moment, revealing more than the words themselves.

Does Inconsistent Speed Speech Mean Emotion Confusion?

When a person's speech alternates unpredictably between fast and slow, it draws immediate attention. *Inconsistent pace* can reflect **inner turbulence, emotional instability, or a deliberate attempt to manipulate the conversation.** Unlike steady rapid speech or consistent delays, fluctuating speed creates a sense of unpredictability that listeners instinctively try to decode.

Emotional instability often manifests in *vocal rhythm*. A person experiencing anxiety, anger, or excitement may unconsciously shift between bursts of rapid speech and moments of pause. These changes mirror the emotional waves beneath the surface, making inconsistent pace a subtle indicator of inner conflict. Listeners may feel unsettled because the voice betrays the lack of equilibrium, even when the words themselves are calm.

However, inconsistency can also be a sign of calculated control. *Skilled communicators* sometimes vary their pace intentionally to **emphasize points, build suspense, or steer emotional responses.** A sudden slow-down can make a statement feel profound, while a rapid burst can create urgency. In these cases, the inconsistency is strategic and accompanied by confidence and congruent body language. The difference between emotional instability and calculated control lies in whether the shifts in pace align with the speaker's intention or seem to arise from uncontrolled impulses.

Cognitive processing also influences inconsistent speech patterns. When someone is formulating complex thoughts or navigating sensitive topics, the brain may alternate between quick expression and careful pauses. This rhythm often appears when a person is balancing truth with self-protection. **The speech becomes a dance between revealing and concealing, and the pace reflects that tension.**

From a listener's perspective, *inconsistent pace* **demands attention because it disrupts predictability.** Human communication thrives on rhythm, and when that rhythm is broken, it signals that something unusual is happening internally. This makes fluctuating speed one of the most revealing aspects of speech patterns in understanding personality and emotional state.

Cultural factors can influence how inconsistency is perceived, but sudden and frequent shifts in pace tend to stand out universally. They hint at either heightened emotion or intentional manipulation, both of which provide insight into the speaker's motives and state of mind. Observing not just the pace itself but also the *moments* when it changes offers valuable clues. Does the speech speed up when a *sensitive subject* arises? Does it slow dramatically before delivering critical information? These patterns often say more than the words being spoken.

Ultimately, inconsistent pace sits at the **intersection of authenticity and performance.** When it stems from emotional instability, it reveals the speaker's vulnerability and lack of internal balance. When it is the result of calculated control, it showcases awareness of communication as a tool for influence. In both cases, it serves as a powerful indicator of what lies beneath the surface of spoken words.

If Someone Puts Their Phone Face Down, They Are Likely Hiding Something

The Power Behind Small Gestures

And every small gesture tells a bigger story.

In the modern era, the smartphone has become an extension of the human mind. It stores personal conversations, intimate details, and private moments. Because of this, how a person handles their phone often reveals more about them than they realize. One subtle but telling behavior is the act of placing a phone face down during a conversation or social interaction. On the surface, it may appear to be a neutral or polite gesture, but beneath this simple movement lies a wealth of psychological and social cues.

The Psychology of Placing a Phone Face Down

When someone places their phone face down, they are actively restricting the visibility of notifications, messages, and calls. This behavior creates a physical barrier between their private digital world and the surrounding environment. The question arises: why would someone feel the need to create such a barrier?

According to psychology, if someone puts their phone face down when they are sitting across from you, it is likely they are hiding something they don't want you to know. Often, the answer points to concealment. It is a signal that there is something on the device they do not want to expose, whether consciously or unconsciously.

Placing a phone face down can be interpreted as an act of control. In that moment, the individual decides to manage how much of their private life is visible to others. This behavior becomes especially revealing when the person does it automatically, without being asked to silence their phone or put it away. The subconscious nature of this habit often speaks louder than words. It is not just about the phone; it is about what the person is trying to keep hidden.

Hiding beyond phones: a story

But this kind of hiding isn't limited to phones. It happens everywhere—in daily behavior, in subtle movements, in small tricks to conceal truth. Here's a story. I once went to a restaurant with a friend—someone I consider unusually observant. We ordered a dish, and when it arrived, we noticed something unexpected: a dead fly floating in the soup. I immediately reached for my phone to call the waiter, but my friend gently stopped me.

Instead, he took a few coins from his pocket—quietly, casually—and dropped them into the bowl. Not in a loud or dramatic way. He simply tilted the bowl slightly, slid the coins in so they sank to the bottom, and then placed the bowl neatly back on its plate. The coins were now completely hidden.Then he called the waiter and said politely, "Excuse me, there's a fly in this. Would it be possible to get a fresh one? " The waiter glanced at the bowl, winced, and quickly apologized. "Of course, sir. Right away."He took the bowl and disappeared into the kitchen.

A few minutes later, a steaming new bowl was placed in front of us. The waiter smiled and left without a word.My friend didn't touch the soup.Instead, he slowly lifted the bowl, looked underneath and smiled.The same coins were still there.The soup hadn't been replaced. Only the surface had changed.The waiter had removed the visible problem, but not the deeper truth.
My friend turned to me and said quietly:

"When people think you're not watching, that's when they hide the most."

What This Story Teaches Us

This wasn't just about a dishonest restaurant. It was about human behavior.

Hiding isn't always loud. Sometimes it's polite, smiling, and dressed in customer service.

The same principle applies when someone flips their phone face down. The gesture may seem small, almost considerate — but it can be a signal. A message left unread, a notification unseen, a truth left submerged under the surface.

What made this moment powerful wasn't the confrontation. It was the preparation.My friend didn't react emotionally. He anticipated the lie — and made it visible.He didn't need to raise his voice or accuse anyone. The coins did the talking.

Not Always Deception: The Polite Side

Not all cases of placing a phone face down stem from deception. In some situations, people do it to demonstrate attentiveness. By turning the screen away, they are signaling that they want to focus on the conversation and avoid distractions. This motivation is rooted in respect rather than concealment.

The key to interpreting the act lies in context and consistency. If someone usually keeps their phone upright but suddenly flips it over during a sensitive conversation, the change carries more weight. The sudden shift suggests a heightened need to control information flow in that specific moment.

Body Language and Social Context Clues

Body language accompanying the gesture provides additional clues. A person who puts their phone face down while leaning back or avoiding eye contact may be creating distance both physically and emotionally. Their body is working in harmony with the phone placement to shield something. Conversely, someone who places the phone down with a relaxed posture and maintains open eye contact may simply be attempting to give undivided attention. The act itself is the same, but the surrounding signals shift its meaning entirely.

There is also a social dimension to consider. In group settings, placing a phone face down can indicate a desire to appear courteous while still maintaining access to private notifications. It is a compromise between being present and keeping personal matters hidden. The behavior becomes more suspicious when combined with other subtle signs: glancing at the phone frequently, quickly flipping it over if it buzzes, or moving it closer to themselves as if guarding it. These micro-actions build a pattern that suggests secrecy rather than mere politeness.

Personality, Culture, and Professional Implications

Psychologically, the act of placing a phone face down can also be linked to boundaries. People who are highly protective of their privacy may do it habitually as a way to maintain control over their personal space. In relationships, this can sometimes create tension. A partner who consistently hides the phone screen, even in casual settings, may inadvertently signal mistrust or secrecy, regardless of their actual intentions. Over time, these small behaviors can shape perceptions and influence the dynamics between individuals.

From an observational standpoint, the timing of the gesture is crucial. If the phone is turned face down immediately upon entering a conversation, it may reflect a general habit of privacy. But if the action occurs at a specific moment — perhaps right after receiving a message or when a sensitive topic arises — it suggests a reactive attempt to conceal information. These subtle shifts reveal the emotional undercurrents driving the behavior.

Technology has amplified the significance of such gestures. In a world where so much personal information lives behind a screen, every movement involving a smartphone becomes part of nonverbal communication. Placing a phone face down is no longer a neutral act; it carries meaning shaped by cultural expectations, personal boundaries, and emotional states. This is why paying attention to these small details can offer insight into what someone may not be saying aloud.

It is also important to consider personality differences. Some individuals are naturally private and guard their devices regardless of circumstance. For them, placing a phone face down may not indicate hiding something specific but rather a general desire to maintain personal boundaries. Others are more transparent and leave their screens visible without concern. Observing how a person behaves over time, across different contexts, helps separate personality-driven habits from situational signals.

In professional environments, the gesture can take on different implications. A colleague who flips their phone over in a meeting may be signaling focus and professionalism, wanting to minimize distractions. However, if the behavior is accompanied by nervous glances or protective body language, it can raise questions about divided attention or hidden priorities. Once again, the act itself is neutral until combined with surrounding cues and emotional context.

Cultural norms also shape interpretation. In some cultures, turning a phone face down is considered a sign of respect and presence, a way to signal that the current conversation is more important than incoming messages. In other cultures, the same act may trigger suspicion, as it implies concealment. Understanding the cultural backdrop is essential when analyzing this behavior, especially in diverse social settings.

Conclusion: The Small Gesture That Speaks Volumes

Ultimately, the gesture of placing a phone face down is a small action that opens a window into larger psychological and social dynamics. It is rarely about the phone itself. Instead, it reflects the individual's relationship with privacy, trust, and control. Observing this behavior alongside other nonverbal cues provides a fuller picture of what the person may be feeling or hiding.

In interpersonal relationships, these subtle signals often accumulate over time, creating patterns that either build trust or raise doubts. A single instance of turning a phone face down may mean little, but repeated instances, especially in sensitive moments, can speak volumes. As with all forms of nonverbal communication, the key is not to jump to conclusions but to look for consistency, context, and accompanying signals.

By paying attention to this seemingly minor act, we gain insight into how people manage their private worlds in public spaces. The phone becomes more than a device; it becomes a symbol of boundaries, trust, and unspoken emotions. In learning to interpret this behavior, we sharpen our ability to read the silent language of modern human interaction.

Because every time a phone is turned over, it tells a story — not just about technology, but about the person holding it.

People Who Flirt a Lot, Lack Love and Attention

Flirting is often perceived as a **playful** and **harmless** act. It can make conversations more exciting, bring warmth to interactions, and even serve as a natural social lubricant. However, when **flirting becomes a frequent and habitual behavior**, it is rarely just about fun or charm. Excessive flirting often reflects an underlying emotional need, **a desire for love and attention** that the person feels is lacking in their life. What appears on the surface as confidence or charisma is sometimes a mask for a much deeper sense of emotional emptiness.

Here's a story:

One crowded morning on a New York City subway, a pregnant woman stepped in. A man offered her his seat. She sat down, no thanks given. A few stops later, she turned with a smug smile and said,

"How old are you?"

"Thirty-two," he replied.

She smirked. "You're five years older than my husband, and he just bought a new car yesterday. Can't believe someone your age still rides the subway."

People around them waited for the man to lash out. But he didn't. Instead, he smiled and said calmly,

"I bought a car too. But my wife is also pregnant, and I'd rather she use it. I'm fine with the subway. But there's no way I'd let my pregnant wife stand on a crowded train."

She went silent. Her eyes stayed on the floor for the rest of the ride.

A few days later, the same man, Jake, was at a wedding reception. A well-dressed woman across the table looked him over and said coldly,

"Too bad I don't have a compliment like that for you."

Jake didn't flinch.

"Don't worry," he replied, "you can always make one up, like I did."

She blinked, stunned, and quietly left to find another table.

These weren't just stories of public restraint.

They were examples of a deeper truth: people who seek attention through mockery, seduction, or arrogance are often trying to fill a void.

Flirting, especially the kind that's compulsive and inappropriate, isn't about affection. It's about validation. It's about desperately trying to feel loved without actually being vulnerable. It's about deflecting from inner emptiness by pulling others into a dance of tension, tease, and control.

But there's power in seeing this clearly.

When you understand that someone's flirtation is not about you — but about what they lack — you stop taking it personally. You stop reacting. You begin observing.

And when you observe long enough, you begin to win — quietly.
You'll learn to spot those who flirt with everyone because they crave the kind of love they never received.
You'll learn to see the difference between charm and manipulation.
You'll learn to stay composed — even when someone is trying to draw you into an emotional game.
Because the calmest person in the room isn't just composed. They're the ones who've already won — by never playing the wrong game.

At its root, flirting is a quest for **validation**. When someone smiles at us, compliments us back, or holds eye contact a little longer than usual, it reassures us that we are seen and valued. **For those who consistently feel deprived of love or emotional support, these moments of attention are like brief drops of water to a parched soul.** The more emotionally starved a person feels inside, the more they may rely on external affirmation to feel worthy. In such cases, flirting is less about genuine romantic interest and more about soothing inner doubts, proving to **oneself that they are desirable and significant.**

Psychologists often note that individuals who engage in constant flirting may have experienced inconsistent emotional nurturing in their formative years. When love and approval were conditional or scarce in childhood, they may develop a pattern of **seeking these feelings in short, immediate doses from external sources.** Flirting offers exactly that: quick bursts of validation that momentarily quiet the deeper insecurities. Over time, this coping mechanism can become a habit, carried into adulthood as a way to **mask an ongoing sense of emotional deprivation.**

It is important to distinguish between *occasional playful flirting* and a *consistent pattern* of it. Lighthearted teasing or mutual attraction is natural and healthy in social dynamics. But when someone seems to flirt with everyone, regardless of context, or needs to maintain constant charm to feel comfortable, it suggests that the behavior is serving a deeper psychological function. **It becomes less about the person they are engaging with and more about feeding their own emotional needs.**

Excessive flirting can also be linked to **self-esteem**. People who **lack steady love and attention** often experience a fragile sense of self-worth. They may depend on the reactions of others to determine how valuable they are. Every smile they elicit or compliment they receive temporarily reinforces their self-image. Unfortunately, this creates a cycle: **the more they flirt, the more they depend on external responses, which can prevent them from developing stable, internal self-worth.**

In relationships, this behavior can become problematic. A partner who constantly flirts with others may not necessarily be unfaithful, but the action can create tension and distrust. Often, they are not seeking romance outside of the relationship but are **chasing the feeling of being noticed and validated.** If they are not receiving enough emotional attention within the relationship — or if their inner void is too deep to be filled easily — they may subconsciously turn to others to meet that need. Understanding this dynamic is essential before labeling the behavior as purely disloyalty; **it is often more about emotional hunger than betrayal.**

Flirting as a substitute for love and attention also reflects how humans cope with loneliness. When people feel unseen or undervalued in their daily lives, they seek small moments of connection wherever they can find them. Flirting becomes a way to create *temporary intimacy*, even if it is superficial. For a few seconds or minutes, they feel noticed, special, and emotionally fed. These fleeting interactions can be addictive precisely because they provide what the person's deeper relationships are failing to deliver.

Another layer to this behavior is *fear of vulnerability*. Seeking love and attention in healthy ways requires openness and emotional risk. It means admitting one's needs and forming deeper connections, which can be frightening for someone who has experienced rejection or neglect. *Flirting, on the other hand, offers a safer route. It provides quick validation without requiring true vulnerability.* The person can receive attention without opening up fully, protecting themselves from potential hurt while still satisfying their craving for emotional nourishment.

Cultural and social factors also play a role. In some environments, distinguish between cultural playfulness and genuine emotional need. However, **the key indicator is the intent and consistency behind the behavior.** Someone who uses flirting as their primary way of connecting with others, regardless of the situation or appropriateness, is likely compensating for an emotional deficit rather than engaging in harmless fun.

Excessive flirting often leaves a pattern in the person's life. Relationships may feel shallow or fail to provide lasting satisfaction because the individual is **constantly seeking the next hit of attention instead of building deep, stable bonds.** Over time, this can create a sense of emotional burnout. The very thing they crave — consistent love and genuine attention — remains elusive because their coping mechanism only offers temporary relief, **not true emotional fulfillment.**

It is crucial to **approach this topic with empathy** rather than judgment. People who flirt a lot are not always manipulative or insincere. More often, they are carrying unmet emotional needs that **they do not fully understand themselves.** Their behavior is a signal, a subtle call for the love and attention they feel they are lacking. Recognizing this allows us to see beyond the surface charm and **understand the human vulnerability driving it.**

For those who identify this pattern within themselves, self-reflection is the first step. Asking questions like "**What am I really seeking when I flirt?" or "Do I feel valued without external attention?**" can uncover the emotional roots of the behavior. Building a stronger internal sense of self-worth and seeking deeper, more authentic relationships can help break the cycle. **When love and attention are consistently present in one's life, the need to chase them through constant flirting naturally diminishes.**

Ultimately, frequent flirting is less about seduction and more about emotional survival. It is a way for some individuals to cope with the lack of love and attention they desperately crave. Understanding the psychological layers behind this behavior allows us to approach it with compassion and insight, whether we are observing it in others or recognizing it in ourselves. **True healing comes not from chasing fleeting moments of validation but from cultivating lasting connections and learning to feel loved and valued from within.**

Chapter 4

Contextual Insights

Drinking to See People's Hearts

Why alcohol unmasks the emotions we hide

They say if you want to know someone's true nature, watch them when they're drunk. Whether at a party, a wedding, or a quiet night among friends, **alcohol has a way of disarming the mind's defenses** — revealing not just who we are in the moment, but who we've been suppressing for far longer. It dulls the prefrontal cortex — the brain's "brakes" — and brings the emotional brain forward. That's why **how someone behaves under the influence often tells you more than their sober words ever could.**

But drunken behavior isn't random. In fact, it often follows clear emotional patterns. Some people become loud. Others turn hostile. Some collapse in tears. Let's take a closer look at what these behaviors often reveal beneath the surface.

Loud When Drunk: Repressed in Daily Life

Some people seem to come alive after a few drinks — their voices rise, their laughter becomes infectious, and their presence fills the room. But these aren't always the extroverts of the group. In fact, this transformation often occurs in people who are **emotionally restrained in daily life.**

In psychological terms, these individuals are often **high in self-monitoring** — they pay close attention to how they're perceived, carefully managing their words, gestures, and emotional expressions. In work or family life, they may appear composed, polite, even distant. But under the influence of alcohol, those mental filters drop — and the **suppressed need for expression surges forward.**

That sudden loudness is more than volume — it's **emotional release.**

They might:

- Talk more than usual
- Interrupt others with bursts of energy
- Laugh uncontrollably or share deeply personal stories

This behavior isn't just "being drunk" — it's **a window into what's been held in**: the jokes unsaid, the opinions stifled, the vulnerability buried under daily responsibility.

> *The louder someone becomes when drinking, the more silent they may have felt when sober.*

Alcohol gives permission — for some, it's permission to finally take up space.

Aggression After Alcohol: A Sign of a Fiery Temper

Not all transformations are joyful. For some, alcohol turns smiles into scowls, and small slights into full-blown confrontations. **Alcohol-related aggression** is one of the most well-documented behavioral shifts — and often one of the most dangerous.

But what causes it?

From a neurological perspective, alcohol **impairs impulse control** while heightening emotional reactivity. This is a potent mix — especially in people who already struggle with:

- Anger regulation
- Low frustration tolerance
- Feelings of powerlessness or inadequacy

For these individuals, alcohol becomes a **disinhibitor**, exposing a temper that's usually kept under wraps. The aggression may be triggered by minor events — a misinterpreted comment, a glance, or even someone taking "too long" at the bar.

And it's not always physical. Verbal outbursts — sarcasm, insults, passive-aggressive digs — may also emerge in people who typically suppress conflict. In relationships, this kind of behavior can be emotionally damaging, often followed by apologies or denial the next day.

So, is alcohol the problem — or is it revealing the problem? The answer is both. While alcohol doesn't create traits from nothing, it can **amplify underlying emotional patterns**:

- **A controlling personality may become possessive.**
- **A person with envy may pick fights over status.**
- **A resentful partner may say what they've held back for years.**

Alcohol doesn't insert anger — it removes the mask that keeps it hidden.

If someone becomes consistently aggressive after drinking, it's rarely "just how they are drunk." It's often **a glimpse of unresolved emotional volatility.**

Crying When Drunk: Emotionally Overwhelmed or Unresolved Trauma?

Tears and alcohol have long been close companions. For some people, the moment they reach a certain level of intoxication, the tears begin — sometimes quietly, sometimes in full emotional collapse.

This reaction is often misunderstood. On the surface, it may look like weakness or instability. But in reality, **drunk crying is one of the clearest signs of unresolved emotional pain.**

When sober, we're taught — and often forced — to keep it together. Pain is tucked away for later, "dealt with" by distraction or denial. But alcohol **removes the mental gatekeepers** that block access to those deeper emotional wounds. Suddenly, the memories, regrets, or buried grief come rushing forward.

Drunk crying can be triggered by:

- **A song** that stirs memories
- **A friend's comment** that hits a nerve
- **A moment of loneliness** in the middle of a crowd

For some, the crying feels out of nowhere — but it never is. The emotion has been there all along, **just waiting for the silence to break open.**

In therapeutic terms, crying while drunk may signal:

- **Unprocessed trauma**
- **Chronic emotional suppression**
- **Long-standing grief or heartbreak**

It's important to note that **not all tears are negative.** Some people cry out of **emotional overflow** — joy, nostalgia, relief, or even love. But when the tears return over and over after drinking, especially in intense or sobbing forms, it may point to **emotions that are asking — or begging — to be felt.**

Sometimes, alcohol is the only moment the body feels safe enough to finally cry.

So What Does Alcohol Actually Reveal?

In many ways, **alcohol is a mirror**, but a warped one. It doesn't show us the full truth, but it often shows us **the hidden chapters.**

- **Loudness** reflects suppressed expression.
- **Aggression** reflects unhealed anger or dominance struggles.
- **Crying** reflects emotional overload or buried wounds.

But this isn't about labeling people by their drinking behavior — it's about asking **why those behaviors surface when the mind's guard is down.**

If someone's drunk self seems wildly different from their sober self, it's worth wondering:

- Are they holding too much inside?
- Do they feel seen in their daily life?
- What pain are they protecting the world from?

Understanding what alcohol reveals isn't about blame — it's about empathy. Because beneath the noise, the rage, or the tears, there's almost always **a human heart that wants to be heard.**

What Clothing Says About Personality

Every outfit is a message. Are you reading it right?

Clothing is more than just fabric — it's a language. Whether consciously or unconsciously, people **signal personality traits, emotional needs, and social intent** through what they wear. From bold colors to subtle tailoring, every choice sends a cue about **how a person sees themselves and how they want to be seen.**

Here's a story:

A sharply dressed woman stepped into a high-end sports car showroom. Tailored coat, heels that clicked with confidence, and a presence that silenced the room. She didn't browse. She didn't hesitate.

She locked eyes on the sleekest machine and asked,

"How much?"

"Two hundred thousand," the salesperson replied.

She nodded. "I'll take it."

As the paperwork was being prepared, she paused—one brief, human moment.

"Am I being reckless?" she asked softly.

Now imagine you're the salesperson. Say it's not risky, and she may think you're desperate to close the deal. Say it is, and she might walk away.
But this salesperson didn't flinch.
He smiled and said:
"Ma'am, when you drive this down the street, people will stare in admiration—but only you get to own it. The rest can just dream."
She laughed. Handed him her card.
Deal closed.
Was it about the car? Not really.
It was about identity.
It was about what she was wearing, how she carried herself, and what that signaled: decisiveness, independence, elegance—but still a lingering need for reassurance.
Because clothing is never just about fashion.
It's a language, one we speak before we say a word.

When someone walks into a room, you already know if they feel powerful, insecure, lost, or in control — just by how they're dressed. And no, it's not about brands or price tags. It's about choices. A crisp white shirt with minimal accessories? Likely someone who values clarity and control. Loud patterns and bold jewelry? Possibly craving attention — or celebrating their inner fire. Sloppy clothes in a professional setting? Maybe they're feeling overwhelmed or disenchanted. **What we wear betrays us before we have a chance to protect ourselves with words.** And people who understand this — leaders, lovers, salespeople, negotiators—use it to their advantage. Not to judge. But to read. To understand who they're dealing with — and to adapt accordingly.

That's why the best salespeople don't just sell products. They read personalities — and reflect back what people want to feel. Not what they say. What they need. **This article isn't about fashion. It's about how to read people through their choices — starting with their clothes.** Because behind every outfit is a desire :

- **To impress.**
- **To disappear.**
- **To dominate.**
- **To protect.**
- **To belong.**

And once you learn to decode that...You'll never walk into a room blind again.

In this article, we explore three revealing patterns: the connection between flashy clothes and self-image, how color reflects inner emotion, and what someone's style says about their core identity.

The More Fancy the Clothes, the Stronger the Desire to Show Off

We all know someone who dresses to impress — elaborate patterns, designer logos, or perfectly polished details from head to toe. But what drives that? Often, it's not just about aesthetics — it's about **identity projection.**

In psychology, this connects with the idea of **impression management** — the way people control how others perceive them. When someone goes out of their way to dress in an exaggerated or flashy manner, especially in casual or inappropriate contexts, it may signal:

- **A need for external validation**
- **Status anxiety or insecurity**
- **A desire to assert dominance or superiority**

The fancier the outfit, the louder the message:

> *"Look at me. I matter. I'm important."*

But there's nuance here. Flashy dressing doesn't always mean arrogance — it can also stem from:

- Growing up in environments where appearance equaled safety or respect
- Feeling invisible in daily life and using clothing to be seen
- Associating self-worth with success symbols like luxury brands

That said, if someone consistently **overdresses relative to their environment**, or shifts dramatically based on who they're around, it may point to **a fragile sense of identity** — one that's built more on others' eyes than internal clarity.

Bottom line: Fancy clothes are not the issue. It's the *need behind the outfit* that reveals who someone really is.

Judging People by the Color of Their Clothes

Color speaks. Before someone opens their mouth, their color choice has already whispered a message. Psychologists have long studied the emotional impact of color, and when it comes to fashion, it can be a surprisingly accurate emotional indicator.

Let's break down a few common ones:

Red: Confidence, energy, sensuality, or a desire to dominate. People who wear red often want to be noticed — or want to *feel* more powerful than they currently do.

Black: Authority, seriousness, or emotional shielding. It's sleek and safe — the go-to for those who want to look sharp while staying protected.

White: Cleanliness, simplicity, or the need to feel fresh and in control. Also used in situations where someone wants to reset or re-center emotionally.

Blue: Calm, stability, and reliability. Those who wear blue often seek to build trust or exude a sense of groundedness.

Yellow or orange: Warmth, optimism, or a desire to connect. But excessive use can sometimes hint at **anxiety behind the smile** — the attempt to radiate light while hiding personal darkness.

Green: Balance, nature, and harmony. People who favor green tend to crave peace — either internally or in relationships.

Gray: Emotional neutrality, indecision, or attempts to blend in. Overuse may indicate **emotional fatigue** or **social withdrawal.**

Of course, color choice can also be cultural, seasonal, or trend-driven. But over time, patterns emerge. If someone consistently dresses in **dark, heavy tones**, it may reflect emotional withdrawal or guardedness. If someone wears

bright, clashing colors, it might signal expressive energy — or emotional chaos.

> *Color is the emotional volume of an outfit. The louder or quieter it is, the more it says.*

Judging People by Their Clothing Style

Style is different from fashion. Fashion is **what's trending**; style is **what's consistent.** It's the fingerprint of someone's visual identity. Whether minimalist, sporty, vintage, or chaotic, the way someone assembles an outfit often tells you more than words ever could.

Let's explore some personality clues behind common styles:

1. Minimalist Dressers
Neutral colors, clean lines, no logos — just simplicity and elegance.

- Likely traits: **Logical, self-contained, emotionally disciplined**
- These individuals often seek control and mental clarity. They dislike drama, both in life and in aesthetics.
- Their style says: "*I know who I am. I don't need to prove it.*"

2. Athleisure & Sporty Looks

Function first, comfort second. But always polished.

- Likely traits: **Energetic, driven, goal-oriented**
- These are people who value **performance and movement** — and often apply the same to life. They like momentum, hate stagnation.
- Their style says: "*I'm always in motion — physically and mentally.*"

3. Bohemian / Artistic Styles

Patterns, layers, unusual textures, and non-mainstream brands.

- Likely traits: **Creative, emotionally intuitive, nonconformist**
- These people often reject social norms and use style as **a canvas for emotional or ideological expression.**
- Their style says: "*Don't put me in a box — I live outside the lines.*"

4. Luxury / Brand-Heavy Dressers

Clear logos, luxury items, hyper-styled outfits.

- Likely traits: **Status-conscious, ambitious, possibly insecure**
- This style can either reflect true confidence — or a need to project confidence where it lacks internally.
- Their style says: "*I deserve attention. I've earned visibility.*"

5. Vintage / Retro Aesthetics
Nostalgic choices, older silhouettes, or period-specific influences.

- Likely traits: **Romantic, sentimental, reflective**
- These people may be deeply attached to memory, meaning, or identity. The past comforts them — or defines them.
- Their style says: "*Time moves forward, but I dress in what feels timeless*."

6. Chaotic / Mixed Styles
No clear rules — clashing colors, textures, or unexpected combinations.

- Likely traits: **Emotionally intense, spontaneous, possibly anxious**
- Style here becomes **a mirror of emotional flux.** The outfit changes with the inner weather.
- Their style says: "*I feel everything, and I wear all of it.*"

Final Thoughts:
Clothing as Emotional Architecture

Clothing is not shallow. It is **structured self-expression** — a daily decision that reflects emotion, desire, insecurity, and identity. When you look at what someone wears, you're looking at:

- Their relationship with attention
- Their emotional needs that day
- Their values — spoken and unspoken
- Their unexpressed longings

Before you hear a person speak, their clothing has already told you a story.

So instead of asking, "Why are they dressed like that?" — a better question might be:"**What do they need to feel like themselves today?**"

How to Know If Your Crush Likes You

Reading the hidden cues of attraction

When it comes to attraction, most people don't confess their feelings directly — they reveal them indirectly, through body language, tone, and behavior changes. The human brain is wired to protect itself from rejection, so signs of interest are often subtle, even unconscious. But once you know what to look for, you'll start to notice the signals beneath the surface.

This article explores three common — but often overlooked — signs that someone might like you more than just a friend: mirroring your movements, blushing during conversation, and suddenly becoming more talkative around you.

Mirroring: A Subtle Sign of Attraction

When someone likes you, their body starts to agree with yours — without saying a word.

One of the most reliable (and research-backed) signs of subconscious interest is mirroring — the natural tendency to copy another person's posture, gestures, speech rhythm, or movements. This happens because of the mirror neuron system in the brain, which helps us feel connection and empathy.

When someone likes you, their brain wants to sync up — and it often does so through physical mimicry.

Examples of mirroring:

- You cross your arms; a few seconds later, they do the same.
- You lean forward; they lean in too.
- You touch your hair, and they suddenly adjust their clothes.
- Your tone speeds up, and theirs matches the pace.

Importantly, mirroring isn't conscious. People aren't trying to impress or imitate — their nervous system is simply aligning because it feels emotionally invested. Mirroring creates psychological closeness, and studies show it builds trust faster than direct conversation.

How to test this: Try changing your posture subtly — lean

back, tilt your head, shift your position — and see if they do the same within 10–20 seconds. If they consistently mirror you, especially when you're not facing each other directly, it could be a nonverbal clue of connection.

Attraction doesn't always speak — it reflects.

When a Group Is Laughing: The Unspoken Signal

One revealing moment happens during group laughter. **When a group of people is laughing, everyone will suddenly look at the one they are most interested in.** This fleeting collective glance often highlights the person who holds the group's emotional focus or romantic interest. It's a subconscious cue showing who captures attention and curiosity.

Blushing While Talking — Is It a Sign of Inner Anxiety?

Sometimes, the face speaks what the mouth can't.
Blushing is one of the most involuntary emotional reactions we have. It's controlled by the sympathetic nervous system and triggered by social attention, embarrassment, or romantic arousal. If someone blushes around you, especially when you're speaking to them or complimenting them, it's a powerful sign of emotional sensitivity.

But does blushing mean they like you? Not always — but it often means they care what you think.

Blushing around a crush can mean:

- They're self-conscious because they want to impress you.
- They're nervous about how they come across.
- They feel emotionally exposed when engaging with you.

For shy individuals, blushing might occur more easily — and more intensely — around people they're attracted to. You might notice:

- A sudden reddening of the cheeks, ears, or neck.Downward glances or nervous fidgeting after a compliment, Laughing, then looking away quickly

In romantic psychology, blushing is a sign of vulnerability — and attraction often requires that vulnerability to take root. If someone blushes often around you but not others, it may point to a deeper emotional reaction tied to your presence.

You can fake words. You can fake gestures. But you can't fake a blush.

Talking More Than Usual: Trying to Build a Connection

When someone talks more around you, they're not just filling space — they may be building a bridge. One of the strongest indicators of romantic interest is a noticeable increase in communication efforts. People who are typically quiet might suddenly become chatty around their crush. Those who are already social might focus their attention more heavily on you — asking deeper questions, sharing personal stories, or trying to keep the conversation going even when it starts to fade.

What drives this behavior?

Desire for connection — Talking is a way to create emotional intimacy. When someone talks more around you than around others, it often means they're trying to establish rapport or test compatibility.

- Anxiety relief — Some people talk more when nervous. They may ramble, overshare, or fill silences because they're worried awkwardness will "ruin the moment."
- Hidden excitement — Increased talkativeness can stem from genuine joy at your presence — their brain is activated, their dopamine is flowing, and their words follow.

Signs this talkativeness is attraction-based:

- They ask open-ended questions to keep you talking
- They circle back to previous conversations ("You mentioned last week you like ____...")
- They seem unusually animated or expressive when you're around.

Even someone who is socially confident may "turn it up" around a person they like. If their energy, tone, or word count noticeably increases with you — especially if they don't behave that way with others — you may be the emotional focus in that space.

When someone talks more than usual around you, it's not just noise. It's intention in disguise.

A Quick Recap: Hidden Signs to Watch For

- Mirroring reveals subconscious connection and emotional alignment.
- Blushing reflects emotional vulnerability and deep self-awareness.

Extra talkativeness signals a desire to connect — or a brain trying to impress. None of these signs guarantee romantic interest, but when they appear consistently — and especially when they're different from how that person acts with others — they're often worth trusting.

Most people don't say how they feel — not with words. They say it through shifts in energy, eye contact, nervous gestures, and changes in how they show up. Attraction isn't always loud — but it's usually visible if you know where to look.

How People Behave When They Lie

Not all lies are told with words — most are told with the body.

We all lie — whether to protect someone's feelings, avoid punishment, or shape how others see us. But while words can be carefully chosen, the body often betrays what the mind wants to conceal. That's why the most skilled lie detectors don't just listen — they watch.

Lying creates psychological discomfort. The brain, especially the prefrontal cortex, must work harder to fabricate, suppress guilt, and stay consistent. This cognitive overload often leaks into micro-behaviors, like body shifts, speech patterns, and facial cues.

Here's a story:

It was one of the most devious cons ever pulled off.

A trap so subtle, it didn't just fool people—it made them complicit.

Back in the early 1900s, during the post-Gold Rush era, a clever entrepreneur bought a stretch of useless, overgrown land in Northern California. He told people he wanted to build a vineyard. But that was only part of the truth.

He needed laborers. But no one in town wanted to work—too lazy, too proud. Even when wages were tripled, workers lounged in the shade, barely lifting a shovel.

They laughed behind his back. "What a fool," they said. "That land's worthless."

Until, one day, a worker's shovel hit something solid. A metallic clink.

The man secretly pocketed what looked like gold.

Another man unearthed a nugget and ran off with it.

The boss? He saw it all—and said nothing.

Instead, he gathered everyone and said:

"Today's your last day. You'll be paid in full. Leave and never return."

Confused, the workers left.

But that night, they crept back—shovels in hand, eyes wild with greed.

They dug under moonlight. They fought over dirt.

Word spread. Strangers came pouring in, chasing dreams of hidden gold.

What no one knew was this:

The gold was fake.

Tiny nuggets of gold-plated lead, carefully buried by the

businessman himself.

In three days, the entire land was cleared—for free.

And the lying? It wasn't just from the man who buried fake gold.

It was in the way the workers lied to themselves:

> "I'm not stealing—I found it fair and square."
>
> "This land must be full of treasure."
>
> "Everyone else is doing it—why not me?"

But when arrests began and lawsuits followed, their justifications fell apart.

Some tried to return the gold—only to discover it was worthless.

Many were forced into indentured contracts to pay damages.

The businessman didn't just win.

He created a workforce, built an empire, and was later celebrated as a local hero.

That's the most dangerous kind of lie—the one people want to believe.

When people lie, they don't always raise red flags.

They don't always sweat, avoid eye contact, or trip over their words.

Often, the most convincing liars say very little. They let you fill in the blanks. They let you create the story, the fantasy, the justification. And when you want something badly enough — status, love, success, a shortcut you'll do what the workers did: Lie to yourself before anyone else has to.

This article isn't just about spotting lies in others.
It's about recognizing the subtle behaviors that emerge when people deceive:

- The overconfident pause before answering a simple question
- The too-specific details that feel oddly rehearsed
- The fake vulnerability designed to distract you from motive
- The shifting blame, the passive "I didn't mean to"s, the performative guilt

It teaches you how to read between the lines — not just with your ears, but with your eyes and intuition.

Because in business, relationships, and everyday life, you're surrounded by carefully crafted illusions.The smiling colleague who undermines you behind closed doors. The charming partner who hides things in plain sight. The polite salesperson who bends facts without technically lying.If you've ever walked away from a situation feeling like something was off — but couldn't quite explain why — this article is your answer .

Understanding how people behave when they lie doesn't make you cynical. It makes you powerful.
Because once you see the pattern, the illusion breaks.
And in a world full of misdirection, the clearest mind always wins.

Anxious Body Language Often Reveals a Sense of Guilt

The body speaks the truth — especially when the mind tries to lie.

When someone lies, especially if they feel morally conflicted, the tension shows up first in their nervous system. This often translates into anxious physical behavior, even when the person appears verbally calm.

Common signs include:

- Fidgeting — tapping fingers, wringing hands, bouncing knees
- Self-touch — rubbing the neck, scratching the face, playing with jewelry
- Restless feet — pointing away from the listener, tapping nervously
- Shoulder shrugging — particularly when paired with a firm statement ("I didn't take it" + shrug = mixed signals)

These behaviors are often nonverbal self-soothing mechanisms. The liar's body is under pressure — and small movements serve as an unconscious way to reduce internal stress.

But here's the catch: some people are naturally fidgety. So it's not about one gesture — it's about baseline deviation. If someone who is normally calm suddenly can't sit still while answering a simple question, that change is what matters.

Also, context is crucial. Guilt-based anxiety usually creates asymmetrical tension: one hand clenches while the other stays loose; the body leans forward while the legs turn away. This physical "split" often mirrors the psychological conflict of lying. When the words say yes, but the body says "I need to get out of here," trust the body.

A special clue comes from the subtle but telling motions of the arms during moments of discomfort. A special clue comes from subtle arm movements during discomfort. **If someone zones out and you suddenly ask what they're thinking, watch if their arms move towards their bra or nose — this signals they are lying, no matter what they say.**

Fluent Speech — a Sign of Deception

Some liars stumble. Others rehearse.

We tend to think liars stutter, pause, or trip over their words. And while that's often true for spontaneous lies, more experienced or anxious liars may do the opposite: they speak too fluently. Their words flow unnaturally well — polished, rehearsed, and often emotionally flat.

This kind of speech pattern is called verbal overcontrol — when someone tries so hard to avoid mistakes or suspicion that their story becomes too perfect.

Signs of overcontrolled speech:

- Very few pauses or hesitations
- Lack of natural filler words ("uh," "you know," "like")
- Overly detailed timelines or unnecessary information
- Emotionally disconnected tone, even when discussing emotional topics

Why does this happen? Because lying requires active mental effort. The brain is not just recalling — it's creating, editing, and cross-checking in real time. To avoid "slipping up," the person may rely on a script they've mentally rehearsed — which removes spontaneity and vulnerability.

Also, some liars will speak faster than usual, trying to "get through" the lie quickly. Others slow down and speak carefully, hoping to appear more credible. Either extreme — if it deviates from their usual style — can be suspicious.

Truth often stumbles. Lies often glide.

If a person speaks about something serious with mechanical fluency and no emotional breaks, they may not be experiencing the situation — they may be describing a story they invented.

Avoiding Eye Contact: Avoiding the Truth?

One of the oldest "tells" — but not always what you think.

Avoiding eye contact is probably the most famous signal of lying — and yes, it can be meaningful. But it's not always about deception. Sometimes, it's about shame, anxiety, or cultural habit.

Still, in deception studies, liars are more likely to break eye contact during key moments — especially when asked for clarification or caught off guard. Their eyes may:

- Look down or to the side when answering
- Dart quickly instead of holding steady
- Blink excessively during or after speaking

This avoidance often comes from the instinct to retreat. Looking into someone's eyes feels intimate — and lying in that space can be psychologically difficult, especially for people with a conscience.

That said, some skilled liars overcompensate, giving too much eye contact. They "lock eyes" in an effort to appear trustworthy. This is just as unnatural — and often more telling — than avoidance.

What you're looking for isn't eye contact alone — it's mismatch. If someone gives strong eye contact during small talk, but suddenly avoids your gaze when asked about something important, that behavioral switch is the clue.

It's not whether they look at you — it's when they stop.

Putting It All Together: Behavioral Clusters

No single sign proves a lie. But when you see multiple behaviors working together — especially in moments of pressure or questioning — the odds increase dramatically.

- Let's say you ask someone,
  "Did you tell them what I said?"
- They answer:
  "No, I didn't say anything." (spoken quickly, perfectly calm)

While avoiding your eyes, scratching their neck, and shrugging one shoulder

The words are clear — but the body is screaming discomfort. That incongruence is what skilled observers look for.

Lie detection is about patterns, not accusations. And most importantly, it's about consistency — how someone's current behavior compares to their usual self.

Quick Summary: Signs to Watch

- **Anxious body language** (fidgeting, self-touch, asymmetrical movements)
  → Signals internal conflict and guilt-based discomfort.

- **Overly fluent speech** (no pauses, rehearsed tone, too many details)
  → May reflect mental overcontrol and narrative fabrication.

- **Avoidance or overcompensation in eye contact**
  → Indicates fear of exposure or attempts to manage perception.

A Final Thought: Lies Are About Fear

At their core, lies are defense mechanisms — born from fear of consequences, rejection, or shame. People don't just lie to deceive — they lie to protect themselves.

That's why deception isn't always malicious. It's often human. But if you want to know the truth — in any relationship — don't just listen to the words. Watch the shoulders. Track the pauses. Listen to the tone that comes before the answer.

Because sometimes, the silence between sentences tells you everything you need to know.

What Her Movements Secretly Reveal

She may not say it out loud— but her body just did.

When it comes to understanding people — especially in conversations that involve emotion, attraction, or subtle tension — the words someone speaks are just a small part of the message. **The real story is often told through tiny, seemingly meaningless movements.**

Especially in women, nonverbal gestures tend to be **more nuanced**, and often driven by deep emotional undercurrents — whether it's discomfort, disinterest, or emotional resistance.

Here are two small but powerful behaviors that speak volumes — if you know what to look for.

Touching the Earlobe Means She's Bored with the Topic

At first glance, **playing with the earlobe** seems harmless — even charming. But when this gesture shows up in the middle of a conversation, especially one that's been going on for a while, it often signals one thing:

> **She's checked out — politely.**

Touching, tugging, or gently rubbing the earlobe is often a self-soothing behavior. In body language terms, this falls under what psychologists call "pacifying gestures." These are small, repetitive actions the body uses to relieve **low-level discomfort, boredom, or mild social fatigue.**

Why the ear? The earlobe is a sensitive, calming area — and it lies near the vagus nerve, which is connected to the parasympathetic nervous system. Rubbing it can literally **regulate stress** and help the brain cope with disinterest without being rude.

You'll typically see this when:

- The conversation topic feels unrelatable or too one-sided
- She's too polite to interrupt or change the subject
- She wants to disengage, but not confrontationally

Signs it's boredom, not just absentmindedness:

- Done repeatedly during one person's monologue
- Paired with minimal verbal engagement ("Mmm," "Yeah")
- Accompanied by subtle body shifts away — legs turning outward, leaning back slightly

It's not always about you — but it is a signal that **the emotional connection is weakening in that moment.**

When she starts touching her ear, it's probably time to change what you're saying — or how much you're saying.

Nose Touching
Often Signals Distrust or Skepticism

This is one of the most misunderstood gestures in nonverbal behavior. While many people associate **touching the nose** with lying (and it can indicate that), it more often reflects **psychological discomfort, disbelief, or emotional resistance.**

In conversations — especially in emotionally charged or persuasive ones — a quick **rub, scratch, or tap of the nose** may indicate that she's not convinced.

Here's why:

Lying, stress, or hearing something suspicious can activate the body's **fight-or-flight response**, which causes tiny changes in circulation, sweat, and even histamine release. This can make the nose feel **itchy or irritated** — leading to the touch.

But beyond physiology, nose touching is about internal reaction. If she does it while you're:

- Giving an excuse
- Making a promise
- Sharing something overly flattering
- Asking a pointed question
- ...it may signal she's not buying it.

It's also a classic "micro delay" signal.
If she hears something she doesn't like or trust, her hand might briefly go to her nose — almost as if her body is stalling to process the emotional discomfort.

Other signs of skepticism that often accompany nose touching:

- Tightly pressed lips
- Slight head tilt
- One eyebrow raised

- Looking to the side before responding

Her words might say "Okay," but if her hand moves to her nose, it means "I don't fully believe you."

Don't panic if you see this once — but if it happens **at key emotional moments**, especially combined with hesitation or guardedness, it may be time to **slow down and rebuild trust.**

Reading the Signals Together

These two gestures — earlobe touching and nose touching — aren't dramatic, and that's exactly what makes them powerful. Because they're so subtle, they often slip through unfiltered. The person doing them doesn't even realize they're sending a message.

But if you're paying attention, they reveal:

- When she's **disengaging** (earlobe)
- When she's **not convinced** (nose)

Both are invitations — not to confront, but to **reconnect.** Switch topics. Ask what she thinks. Notice how she responds.

Because once the body starts speaking, you'll always learn more than words can say.

Signs of Nervousness in Behavior

The body reveals the stress that words try to hide.

Whether in a job interview, a date, or a difficult conversation, nervousness tends to show itself — not through what we say, but through **how we move.** Our body reacts to psychological stress in deeply ingrained, often unconscious ways. While some people try to look confident, **their nervous habits speak a different truth.**

Here are two powerful behavioral patterns that reveal underlying insecurity or stress, even when the person appears composed on the surface.

Face-Touching, Fidgeting, Adjusting Clothes Are Stress Signals

When someone is nervous, their body looks for ways to cope — and that often shows up through **excessive movement**. These movements are not random. They're forms of **self-soothing**, subtle attempts by the nervous system to calm itself down.

Common nervous behaviors include:

- **Touching the face**: rubbing the nose, scratching the cheek, touching the chin
- **Fidgeting**: tapping fingers, shifting weight, bouncing legs, clicking pens
- **Adjusting clothes**: tugging on sleeves, smoothing the collar, checking buttons or jewelry

These behaviors are typically unconscious — the person isn't trying to be deceptive or awkward. Instead, their brain is under mild stress, and the body compensates by releasing tension through movement.

This cluster of behaviors is often seen:

- Right before someone speaks in public
- During moments of confrontation or criticism
- When answering a question they're unsure about

- On a first date or during any interaction where they feel they're being "judged"

What makes these behaviors reliable? It's all about **baseline comparison.** If someone is usually calm and still, but suddenly starts adjusting their sleeves every 10 seconds, that's a meaningful shift. Similarly, if someone touches their face repeatedly **only when a certain topic comes up**, it may signal emotional discomfort.

> *The hands will always tell you what the mouth is trying to hide.*

In high-stress environments, these movements may cluster together — for example, someone may laugh nervously, then immediately tug their jacket and rub their nose. The more you notice these patterns, the more clearly you can see when someone feels emotionally unsettled.

Smile Frequently: Hiding Insecurity

Smiling is often interpreted as a sign of warmth, friendliness, or joy. But not all smiles are genuine — and in many cases, **excessive smiling is a defense mechanism.**

When someone smiles too much — especially in situations that don't truly warrant it — it may reflect an internal need to:

- **Mask nervousness**
- **Diffuse perceived tension**
- **Seek approval or avoid conflict**

In psychology, this is sometimes called the "**appeasement smile**." It's a nonverbal way of saying, "Please like me" or "I'm harmless." People who are socially anxious or insecure often develop a habit of **over-smiling** to prevent rejection.

You'll often see this kind of smiling when someone:

- Is trying to make a good first impression
- Doesn't want to appear rude or confrontational
- Is uncertain about how their words will be received
- Is trying to hide nervousness during public speaking or dating

How to spot it:

- The smile appears quickly and disappears just as fast
- It's repeated too often within a short period
- It doesn't match the emotional content of the conversation
- The eyes don't crinkle — a true smile involves the eyes, not just the mouth

When someone smiles while saying "I'm fine," but their shoulders are tense and their eyes dart away — trust the body, not the words.

Frequent smiling isn't always fake — but when it becomes **disconnected from emotional content**, it's usually a sign that the person is trying to **control how they are perceived**, rather than expressing genuine happiness.

Final Thought:
Nervousness Isn't Weakness — It's Data

These small behaviors — touching the face, shifting posture, over-smiling — aren't flaws. They're **emotional indicators**, revealing how someone feels beneath their surface performance.

When you learn to spot nervous cues, you don't just decode anxiety — you learn how to:

- Offer comfort at the right moment
- Choose your words more kindly
- Understand when someone is trying, even if they seem awkward

Because behind every fidget or forced smile is **a human trying to stay safe** in a socially uncertain moment.

The most honest part of a person is the part they're not aware you're watching.

Behavioral Clues of Anxiety

Anxious minds rarely sit still
— and neither do anxious bodies.

Anxiety is not always loud. It doesn't always look like panic attacks or visible shaking. Often, **it whispers through everyday habits** — small, repetitive behaviors that seem normal on the surface, but underneath, reveal **a nervous system under pressure.**

Two of the most common — yet easily overlooked — anxiety-driven behaviors are:

- **Walking faster than necessary**
- **Constantly checking one's phone**

These behaviors often appear in public or semi-social situations — moments where the person **feels exposed, judged, or internally unsettled.**

Let's break them down.

Walking Fast, Checking Phone Constantly: Ways of Avoiding Reality

At first, it seems harmless — even productive. Walking briskly looks like someone is on a mission. But in psychological terms, **unnecessarily fast walking**, especially in calm environments, can be a subtle form of **emotional escape.**

When someone is anxious, their body is operating in a state of **mild fight-or-flight activation.** Their heart rate is up, their muscles are tense, and their mind is scanning for social or emotional threats. In this state, being still or moving slowly **feels unsafe.**

Fast walking serves several functions:

- **Avoiding eye contact or interaction** in public
- **Creating a sense of control** when the mind feels chaotic
- **Physically matching the pace of anxious thoughts**

You'll often see this behavior:

- In hallways, airports, or cafes
- After someone has had a stressful conversation
- When approaching a social setting they're nervous about
- When walking alone in public and feeling "watched"

They're not in a hurry — they just want to get away from a moment they don't feel comfortable in.

This behavior becomes especially telling when paired with:

- Clenched hands or fists
- Stiff posture
- Downward gaze
- No clear destination, yet urgent movement

If someone consistently walks fast in low-pressure situations, it might not be about where they're going — it's about **where their mind doesn't want to be.**

Constantly Checking the Phone: Searching for Escape or Reassurance

We all check our phones. But some people check them **every 30 seconds** — even when there are no notifications. In behavioral psychology, this is known as "**nervous checking**", and it often points to **social anxiety, restlessness, or avoidance.**

Anxiety thrives in silence and stillness. When someone feels uncomfortable — whether they're waiting alone, sitting through awkward small talk, or just unsure how they're perceived — the phone becomes a **safe anchor.**

Why?

Because checking a phone offers:

- **Instant distraction** from internal discomfort
- **A socially acceptable reason** to avoid eye contact
- **A dopamine hit** (the hope that something new is waiting)
- **Reassurance** (checking messages to confirm connection or acceptance)

But here's the paradox:
The more someone checks their phone **without cause**, the more it suggests **they're not mentally present** — not because they don't care, but because they're trying to **soothe internal tension.**

Telltale signs:

- Repeatedly unlocking and relocking the screen
- Scrolling through the same 1–2 apps with no real engagement
- Picking up the phone, looking at it, then putting it down within seconds — over and over
- Using the phone as a buffer between themselves and another person

The phone isn't the focus — it's the escape hatch.

Putting the Two Together: Avoidance in Motion

Both behaviors — walking fast and compulsively checking the phone — are often part of a larger pattern:

Avoidance-based anxiety.

People with this pattern don't always withdraw physically. Instead, they **stay in the environment but mentally detach** through movement and distraction.

It's not "flight" in the traditional sense. It's psychological flight.

They appear "busy."
They seem "on the go."
They're "checking something important."
But in reality, they're using **activity to buffer against emotional discomfort.**

Final Thought: Movement as a Message

If someone walks too fast, too often — ask yourself: *What are they trying not to feel?*

If they keep checking their phone when you talk — consider: *What silence are they trying to avoid?*

Anxiety doesn't always scream. Sometimes it just walks faster and checks the phone again.

How Anger Manifests in the Body

Before anger speaks, the body speaks first.

Anger is not just an emotion — it's a biological preparation for battle. Though society teaches us to stay calm and composed, the body rarely cooperates when anger hits. Even when a person is trying to "act normal," anger sends strong signals through posture, tension, and micro-expressions. Whether it's in the boardroom, the classroom, or across a dinner table, learning to read the physical signs of anger gives you a powerful advantage. It helps you avoid escalation, respond with emotional intelligence, and understand what someone isn't saying out loud.

Let's explore how three major physical cues — clenched fists, a thickened neck, and a locked jaw with furrowed brows — serve as early warning signs of emotional heat rising beneath the surface.

Clenched Fists: Controlled but Intense Rage

One of the most classic, instinctual signs of anger is the clenching of fists. This is not always a precursor to violence — in fact, in modern contexts, it's more often a sign of rage under restraint.

Why it happens:

From a biological standpoint, the moment the brain perceives a threat, real or emotional, it activates the amygdala, triggering the sympathetic nervous system. This fight-or-flight response sends blood to the limbs, tightens muscles, and prepares the body to protect itself. Fist-clenching is part of that package — a subtle form of muscular bracing.

But not all clenched fists mean confrontation is coming. In many cases, it's a sign of emotional regulation — the person is angry, but working hard not to let it out.

Contexts you'll see it:

- During tense conversations, especially when interrupted or disrespected
- While someone is listening to something they strongly disagree with
- In public settings where open anger would be socially inappropriate

What to look for:

- One or both hands forming tight fists without any need to do so
- Knuckles turning pale or red
- Shoulders tensing or elbows locking at the sides
- Minimal hand movement when talking, or arms held rigidly still

Sometimes, the tighter the fist, the harder someone is trying to stay in control.

Also worth noting: clenched fists may appear not just in conflict, but in moments of injustice, humiliation, or frustration. For example, someone passed over for credit or blamed unfairly may clench their fists silently under the table — expressing a form of silent protest.

If someone slams fist on the table... angry or faking

A sudden, forceful slam on the table is a striking signal. It's often interpreted as raw anger — a physical outburst that demands attention or asserts dominance. But sometimes, that slam is *performed* rather than felt. People may exaggerate this gesture to intimidate, manipulate, or feign outrage.

Pay attention to the context and accompanying body language. If the slam is paired with genuine facial tension, furrowed brows, and a flushed face, it likely stems from true anger. However, if the slam feels theatrical or disconnected from emotional cues — such as a forced smile or lack of eye engagement — it could be a calculated display, a form of faking.

Understanding this nuance helps you read not just the action, but the intent behind it.

The Thickening Neck: A Posture of Power and Defense

You may not think of the neck as an expressive part of the body — but it's one of the most viscerally reactive areas during anger.

Ever noticed how a person's neck seems to expand when they're in a heated moment? This is often caused by involuntary engagement of the sternocleidomastoid and trapezius muscles, as well as a slight lift of the shoulders and tightening of the upper spine. Together, these changes create the appearance of a "thickened neck" — a primal dominance and defense display.

Why the neck?

From an evolutionary standpoint, this is about appearing larger and more intimidating. Just as animals raise their fur or puff their chests, humans subconsciously alter posture to ward off threats and assert territory.

In psychological terms, this posture communicates:

- "I am not backing down."
- "You're pushing me too far."
- "I need to defend myself."

Where it shows up:

- In arguments between equals, where a power struggle is taking place
- When someone feels cornered but doesn't want to show fear
- During moments of rising tension in group settings (meetings, family gatherings)

Additional physical signs:

- Shoulder muscles lifting subtly, reducing visible neck length
- Chin raised, head tilted slightly backward (dominance cue)
- Face flushed or jaw jutting forward
- Muscles at the base of the neck visibly pulsing or flexing

A person who "grows taller" in silence may not be trying to win — they're trying not to explode.

Sometimes, the thickening of the neck occurs in micro-form — a quick tightening when someone is triggered, then relaxed again. If you watch closely, these flickers can tell you when a line was just crossed, even if no words were said.

Gritting Teeth and frowning: Instant Release of Anger?

While the body prepares for action, the face works overtime to maintain appearances. But anger often leaks through, especially in two places: the jaw and the brows.

Clenched jaw:

The jaw is home to one of the strongest muscles in the body — the masseter — and it reacts quickly to emotional restraint. When someone is trying not to yell, argue, or cry, the jaw often locks down to keep it all inside.

Signs of jaw clenching:

- The jaw muscle visibly pulsing or bulging
- Teeth grinding silently, especially when not talking
- A flat, horizontal mouth line with the lips pressed tightly
- Speech that sounds unusually tight or clipped

This physical pressure in the jaw is often a substitute for verbal aggression — as if the person is holding their anger with their teeth.

Furrowed brows:

Eyebrows are subtle, but incredibly telling. A deep vertical furrow between the brows, often accompanied by narrowed eyes, indicates mental tension and inner conflict. When anger is layered with confusion, disappointment, or restraint, it shows up here.

You'll often see furrowed brows when:

- A person hears something they feel is unjust
- They're calculating a response but holding back
- They're in emotional pain but don't feel safe expressing it

Paired together — clenched jaw and furrowed brows — these facial cues often indicate "silent explosions": moments when the person is actively suppressing the urge to react. This might happen in:

- Marital arguments
- Professional confrontations
- Situations where someone must maintain image, status, or control

The mouth stays shut. But the face is yelling.

Why Recognizing These Signs Matters

Understanding anger as a physical process — not just an emotional one — can change the way we approach conflict, leadership, and relationships.

When you spot someone clenching their fists, tightening their neck, or locking their jaw, it doesn't mean they're about to lash out. More often, it means they're in a battle with themselves.

By recognizing these signals:

- You can intervene early, de-escalate tension, and create safety
- You can avoid pushing someone past their limit unknowingly
- You can validate what they may not be able to say out loud

Most importantly, you gain empathy. Because anger, at its core, is not always aggression — it's often a protest against pain, injustice, or vulnerability.

Final Reflection: Anger's Body is Loud — Even When the Mouth is Silent

When someone raises their voice, it's easy to notice. But when someone does everything they can to stay calm — and the body starts betraying that effort — that's when real observation begins.

- Look at the hands.
- Watch the shoulders.
- Study the eyes and the jawline.

Because long before anger speaks, it tenses, tightens, and trembles — in silence.

Behavioral Cues of Jealousy

Jealousy doesn't always hiss.
Sometimes it smiles politely and watches too closely.

Jealousy is one of the most complex and hidden emotions in the social world. Unlike anger or sadness, which often have clear physical signals, **jealousy disguises itself.** It rarely announces its presence. Instead, it leaks out through side comments, passive behavior, and mismatched emotions.

What makes jealousy hard to detect — even in ourselves — is that it often hides behind **socially acceptable behaviors**: indifference, humor, even concern. But beneath the surface is a core fear:

> *"I'm not enough compared to them."*

In this article, we'll break down three powerful — and often overlooked — behavioral cues that signal jealousy:

- Pretending not to care

- Subtle comparison
- Sudden, unprovoked criticism

Pretending Not to Care: The Most Common Cover-Up

One of the most frequent signs of jealousy is **emotional withdrawal disguised as disinterest**. Rather than showing visible envy, many people will act like something doesn't matter to them — when in fact, it matters deeply.

This is a form of **emotional self-protection.** By pretending not to care, the person shields themselves from:

- The pain of comparison
- The humiliation of being seen as "less than"
- The vulnerability of openly admitting they want what someone else has

How it looks:

- A friend hears about your promotion and says, "*Oh, that's cool,*" then quickly changes the topic
- Someone scrolls past another person's achievements on social media, saying, "*Good for them,*" but with a cold tone
- A peer shows no reaction when their competitor wins an award, yet seems withdrawn the rest of the day

This "I-don't-care" façade is especially strong when the jealous person **feels socially inferior**. By pretending to be unaffected, they attempt to reclaim power.

Indifference isn't always real. Sometimes it's envy, fully dressed in self-control.

In more private settings, this behavior may shift into **avoidance** — not replying to messages, not attending events, or finding excuses not to engage with the person they feel jealous of.

The emotional logic is simple:

> *"If I don't acknowledge it, I don't have to feel bad about it."*

Comparing Secretly
Is a dissatisfaction of what people owned

Jealousy thrives in the shadow of comparison. But rarely does it look like open competition. Instead, people express jealousy through **low-key comparison behaviors** — trying to quietly measure themselves against others in terms of looks, status, achievement, or attention.

What drives this?

A deep fear of **inadequacy**. Jealousy is not just about wanting what someone else has — it's about **fearing that what you have is no longer good enough.**

Signs of comparison rooted in jealousy:

- Asking pointed questions like, "*So how much did you make this year?*"
- Reacting with visible discomfort when someone receives praise
- Downplaying others' accomplishments by saying things like, "*Well, they had help.*"
- Quickly responding with their own story after someone shares success — a behavior known as "**one-upping**"

You might also see someone **copying another's style, hobbies, or speech patterns** — not because they admire them, but because they feel threatened and want to stay competitive.

Comparison isn't always about curiosity — sometimes it's a sign of inner panic.

In group settings, jealous individuals may engage in **passive performance games** — subtly trying to outdo the other person without making it obvious. For instance, they might suddenly start posting more, dressing better, or name-dropping success stories in shared spaces.

The key emotion here isn't always hatred. It's often **insecurity.** The person doesn't necessarily dislike the one they're jealous of

— they're just **haunted by the thought of not being enough.**

Sudden Criticism: Jealousy in Disguise

Jealousy doesn't always stay silent. When the pressure builds, it often escapes through **criticism — subtle or sharp.**

This usually comes when the jealous person **can no longer maintain the emotional mask.** They start to pick at flaws, question credibility, or **devalue the other person's achievements** — all in an attempt to soothe their own ego.

What it sounds like:

- *"She got that job? That company must be desperate."*
- *"He's not even that talented — he just got lucky."*
- *"Sure, she's pretty, but have you seen how fake she is?"*

In many cases, this type of criticism emerges **out of nowhere,** seemingly unprovoked. That's because the jealous person isn't reacting to something that just happened — they're reacting to **a buildup of inner comparison and resentment.**

It can also appear as:

- "Helpful advice" that's actually meant to cut down the other person

- Laughing at or mocking someone in front of others
- Backhanded compliments *("Wow, I didn't think you could pull that off — good for you!")*

When someone's praise comes wrapped in poison, it's often envy trying to hide.

The function of this behavior is psychological **equalization.** If the jealous person can bring the other down a notch — even just emotionally — they feel better. They feel safer. Less "behind."

Ironically, this kind of criticism is often reserved for **people close to them** — friends, coworkers, even siblings. Jealousy hits hardest when it feels personal, when the success of the other person highlights their own lack.

Why These Signals Matter

Jealousy isn't just an emotion — it's a **behavioral language**. And like all emotions, it communicates something deeper:

> *"I'm afraid I'm falling behind. I'm afraid I don't matter."*

By learning to spot the signals — withdrawal, comparison, criticism — we don't just see jealousy. We see pain, insecurity, and a person struggling to preserve their sense of self-worth.

For those being envied:

- Don't mistake silence for lack of reaction
- Don't take coldness or criticism too personally — it may say more about their fears than about you
- And most importantly, **stay grounded in humility** — nothing calms jealousy like confidence without arrogance

For those feeling jealous:

- Don't suppress it blindly. Get curious about it.
- Ask: What fear is hiding behind this feeling? What belief about myself is being triggered?
- Remember: Jealousy is not a moral failure. It's a mirror.

Final Thought: Jealousy Speaks Through What's Not Said

Most jealous people will never admit it. But their body will. Their tone will. Their actions will.

They won't say they care, but they'll watch closely.

They won't admit comparison, but they'll change their behavior after yours.

They won't say you intimidate them, but they'll find subtle ways to shrink your shine.

Learn to listen — not just to words, but to tone, silence, timing, and microreactions.

Because when jealousy enters the room, it doesn't knock. It hides behind polite smiles, and waits.

How People Show Contempt

Contempt doesn't shout. It smirks, sneers, and scans you like you're beneath them.

Contempt is one of the most corrosive emotions in human interaction — and one of the easiest to overlook. Unlike anger, which often seeks confrontation, or jealousy, which hides, **contempt stands above**. It doesn't want to argue or compete. It wants to **devalue.**

Psychologically, contempt signals a **sense of superiority**. It says:

> *"I'm better than you. I see your flaws, and I'm not impressed."*

Contempt is especially dangerous in relationships — personal, professional, or social — because it doesn't aim to resolve conflict. It aims to **erode respect**. And while many people don't use the word "contempt" in daily life, they often feel it — and more importantly, they often **show** it.

Let's examine three behavioral signals that commonly reveal contempt in everyday interactions:

Scanning from Head to Toe: The Reflection of Superiority

There's a particular kind of look that people give when they feel they're better than someone else — a **slow, deliberate up-and-down gaze**, often followed by a smirk or expressionless face.

This **nonverbal scan** isn't about curiosity — it's about **judgment.**

What it looks like:

- The person looks at your face, then your clothes, shoes, or posture — slowly
- They don't smile or acknowledge you afterward
- The look feels like **you've just been "assessed" and dismissed**

This is what psychologists call a **status check**. In dominant-submissive dynamics, people who feel superior may use this scan to:

- Reinforce **social hierarchy**
- Subtly intimidate or humiliate
- Remind you that you're "being watched" and evaluated

In group settings, you might notice this behavior during:

- Team meetings where power is unspoken but present
- Social events where someone wants to display dominance
- One-on-one conversations where someone is "sizing up" the other person's worth

The head-to-toe scan is the visual equivalent of saying: "You're not on my level."

What makes this dangerous is that the target often feels **unsettled or small**, but can't quite explain why. That's the essence of contempt — **it devalues without confrontation**, leaving the other person confused or defensive.

Frivolous Tone Is Insulting

Contempt doesn't always show in what people say. More often, it leaks through **how they say it.** The most common channel? **A mocking tone.**

Mocking is a form of **passive aggression**. It mimics, exaggerates, or dismisses someone's words, voice, or concerns — not to question them, but to **make them look foolish.**

Examples of mocking tone:

- Repeating what someone just said in a high-pitched or childish voice:
  "*Ohhh, so you're busy now*?"

- Exaggerated sarcasm with rolling eyes:
  "*Wow, what an amazing idea.*"

- Using humor as a cover for judgment:
  "I'm just joking — don't be so sensitive."

Mocking tone often travels with:

- Eye rolls
- Sighing loudly or smirking while someone speaks
- Crossed arms or leaning back with visible disinterest

It's important to distinguish between **playful teasing and contemptuous mockery.** Teasing in healthy relationships involves mutual laughter and consent. Contempt, on the other hand, uses humor as a **weapon**.

- *Mocking is laughter with a blade in it.*

In workplaces, mocking often appears in:

- Dismissive jokes about someone's ideas
- Undermining leadership through tone rather than content

- Calling someone's concerns "dramatic" or "overreacting," especially in front of others

This kind of communication creates a toxic environment where people feel **unsafe to speak** — because what they say might be turned against them, not seriously debated.

Nose Scrunching: Decoding Disgust and Disdain

If you really want to spot contempt early, **watch the nose.**

One of the most consistent micro-expressions associated with contempt and disgust is the **nose scrunch** — a small but distinct wrinkling of the nose, often accompanied by a curled lip.

Why it happens:

In evolutionary psychology, disgust serves a protective function — it tells us to avoid things that might harm us (rotten food, disease, etc.). But in social behavior, **that same disgust reflex** can be triggered toward people — especially when they violate our values or we judge them as "less than."

Nose scrunching may appear:

- When someone is listening to an idea they internally dismiss
- Right after someone says something "cringe" or vulnerable
- When a person is physically present but mentally disgusted

It's a **split-second reaction**, often unconscious, and may be hard to catch unless you're paying attention. Other signs often accompany it:

- Squinting or narrowing of the eyes
- Tilting the head slightly back (as if trying to avoid a bad smell)
- A brief exhale or sigh

They won't say they disapprove. Their nose will.

This expression is particularly common in **hierarchical relationships**, like manager-to-employee or parent-to-child dynamics, when the higher-status individual feels the lower one is making a "foolish" or "unworthy" move.

In romantic relationships, nose scrunching is dangerous — it often signals **deep-seated disgust** that, over time, erodes affection. According to Dr. John Gottman, a leading relationship researcher, contempt (including facial signs like sneers or nose wrinkles) is the **strongest predictor of divorce.**

The Psychology Behind Contempt: More Than Just Ego

So what lies beneath these behaviors? Why do people show contempt?

Most often, contempt is **ego armor**. It's a way of saying:

- *"I don't feel threatened — because I've already decided you're beneath me."*
- *"I don't need to engage — because you're not worthy of real conflict."*

But ironically, contempt usually stems from **insecurity**, not confidence. People express contempt when they:

- Feel challenged by someone they can't openly attack
- Experience envy but refuse to admit it
- Want to assert dominance without exposing vulnerability

This makes contempt a **defensive superiority** — cold, quiet, and corrosive. The person avoids direct fight or flight, and instead chooses **emotional distancing with a sprinkle of insult.**

What to Do When You Notice It

If you're the target:

- **Don't internalize it.** Remember: contempt is often a mirror of the other person's insecurity, not your worth
- **Stay calm, not smaller.** Responding with anger gives them more power
- **Set boundaries.** Contempt thrives in environments where it goes unchallenged
- If persistent — in relationships or workplaces — **name the pattern**, not the person:
  "I notice your tone often shifts when I speak. Is something bothering you?"

If you catch yourself doing it:

- Get curious: *What am I afraid to feel? What am I protecting?*
- Replace the scan with listening, the smirk with a question, the judgment with empathy
- Contempt may protect the ego, but it **destroys connection**

Final Thought: Contempt Is a Quiet Violence

Contempt doesn't break windows. It doesn't shout. It **undermines.**

It tells the other person, "*You're not worth basic respect.*" And over time, that message — whether shown through looks, tone, or expressions — can do real damage.

But here's the truth:

> *The need to look down on others often comes from fear of being looked down upon.*

Recognizing contempt in others — or in ourselves — isn't about blame. It's about awareness. And awareness is the first step to shifting from superiority to **true confidence**.

Because truly strong people don't need to mock, scan, or sneer. They know their worth — and they don't need to shrink others to prove it.

Chapter 5

Reading People Through Their Responses

Physical Responses to Intense Fear

Fear doesn't always scream. Sometimes, it stares. Sometimes, it freezes. Sometimes, it trembles just beneath the skin.

Fear is one of the most primal emotions humans experience. Long before we could put our feelings into words, our bodies were already fluent in the language of survival: fight, flight, or freeze.

But when fear reaches an intense level — the kind that bypasses logic and hijacks the nervous system — the body reacts in unmistakable ways. These reactions are not random; they are **deeply wired signals** that once kept our ancestors alive.

Let's explore the four most revealing physical signs of **intense fear**, what they mean, and how to recognize them in ourselves and others.

Dilated Pupils: The Body's Escaping Signal

When someone is afraid, their pupils often dilate — becoming wider and darker. This isn't just a coincidence. It's one of the fastest and most automatic responses in the human body.

Why it happens:

- In threatening situations, the sympathetic nervous system kicks in.
- Pupils dilate to let in more light, improving visual clarity and **expanding peripheral vision** — helping the body spot escape routes or approaching threats.
- *In fear, your eyes aren't just looking — they're scanning for survival.*

This dilation can happen:

- Within seconds of a perceived threat
- Even if the person remains outwardly calm
- Whether the fear is physical (a threat in the environment) or emotional (confrontation, exposure, rejection)

What it reveals:

- The body has entered **hyper-alert mode**

- Even if the person says they're "fine," their eyes may tell a different story
- It's not always conscious — many people don't even realize their pupils have changed

In human interaction, dilated pupils may show up during:

- Sudden anxiety or panic
- Fear of being caught, exposed, or judged
- The moment just before fleeing or freezing

Frozen in Place: Paralyzed by Fear

Perhaps the most misunderstood fear response is **freezing** — the inability to move or speak when danger is present.

People often expect fear to produce action — screaming, running, fighting. But many fear responses lead to **immobility.**

Freezing is not failure. It's evolution.

Why the body freezes:

- From an evolutionary standpoint, stillness once protected us from predators.

- Some threats (like large animals) were more likely to ignore us if we appeared non-responsive.
- Modern threats (emotional conflict, public shame, sudden shock) still trigger this **neurobiological shutdown**.

How it appears:

- Standing or sitting still with little movement
- Blank facial expression, "zoning out"
- Lack of speech or delayed responses
- Muscle tension without motion

Freezing is especially common in:

- Victims of trauma
- Socially anxious individuals during performance or conflict
- Children during yelling or physical punishment

While freezing may be silent, it reflects **a loud internal alarm.** The body is caught between danger and decision, **unable to choose a safe path.**

Trembling Voice: On the Edge of Depressing Fear

One of the most telling fear indicators is **what happens to the voice**. When someone is trying to speak while afraid, the body betrays them.

The vocal cords tighten. Breathing becomes shallow. The voice cracks, trembles, or hesitates.

Common signs:

- Shaky tone, especially at the beginning of sentences
- Words breaking mid-phrase due to irregular breath
- Speeding up speech to "get it over with"
- Repeated throat-clearing or swallowing
- *When the voice shakes, it's not weakness. It's the body pushing through fear.*

This happens when:

- Someone is speaking up in an unsafe environment
- A person fears being judged, rejected, or punished for what they're saying
- Emotional overload overwhelms the ability to regulate speech

In public speaking, this is often called **stage fright**, but in deeper emotional contexts — like a confrontation, confession, or vulnerable moment — it reflects a core internal battle.

The person is caught between:

Silence (safety)

And speech (truth)

Their body is asking: "*Can I survive this moment of exposure?*"

When The Body Tightens up, it's A Sign of Escaping

Another clear marker of intense fear is **physical contraction** — when the body literally tightens in on itself.

You'll see:

- Arms folded tightly across the chest
- Shoulders raised and drawn inward
- Hands clenched or gripping the nearest object
- Neck pulled down, jaw locked, legs stiff or crossed tightly

The body is trying to shrink — to become smaller, less visible, harder to hurt.

This isn't just about anxiety. It's the body's way of signaling "**retreat.**"

It often shows up right before:

- Someone withdraws emotionally or physically from a situation
- They give up on expressing themselves
- They shut down in arguments, interviews, or intimate settings

What's happening internally:

- The body is preparing for **social escape**
- The mind anticipates rejection, judgment, or harm
- Muscles tense as a **barrier** between self and environment

In some cases, people don't even realize they're doing it. Their body's fear system is acting **faster than conscious awareness.**

Fear Is Intelligent — But Not Always Accurate

These physical signs evolved to keep us alive — and in true life-threatening danger, they're incredibly effective.

But in modern life, **emotional threats** often feel just as intense as physical ones. A job interview, a breakup conversation, a vulnerable confession — the body may respond as if it's being hunted.

The problem?

The body can't always tell the difference between:

- Real danger vs. emotional discomfor
- Actual attack vs. imagined judgment
- Present moment vs. past trauma echoing forward

That's why many people experience:

- **Fear responses during safe moments**
- Overreactions that confuse both them and those around them
- Shame about freezing, trembling, or withdrawing — as if these were character flaws

How to Support Someone in Fear (Or Yourself)

Whether you're observing someone else's fear — or recognizing it in yourself — the key is **not to push or shame** the reaction.

Instead:

- **Create psychological safety**
  "Take your time. You don't have to speak until you're ready."
- **Soften your presence**
  Slow your voice. Lower your intensity. Remove pressure.

- **Normalize the reaction**
  "It's okay to feel nervous. It makes sense."

- **Offer grounding tools**
  Breathing techniques, anchoring with physical objects, naming emotions out loud

Fear softens when it feels safe. Not when it's told to disappear.

Final Thought: The Body Doesn't Lie — It Protects

Fear may not always make sense to the outside world. But to the person experiencing it, it's real. Their body believes something is at stake — and it's trying to help.

So when someone's eyes dilate... when their voice trembles... when they freeze or shrink...

> Don't ask: "*What's wrong with you?*"
> Ask: "*What happened to you?*"
> Or even better: "*What are you protecting yourself from right now?*"

Because every **physical fear response is a kind of wisdom** — it tells us not just what's frightening, but what matters.

And that is always worth noticing.

The Body's Reaction to Threats

Before the mind decides, the body already knows.

When we sense a threat — physical, emotional, or social — the body doesn't wait for conscious permission. It **reacts**. Muscles shift. Posture tightens. Movements shrink.

These reactions happen in milliseconds, often **before we even realize we're afraid.** They're not flaws or signs of weakness. They're ancient survival patterns — physical expressions of the brain saying:

> *"This might not be safe."*

Let's break down three of the most subtle yet telling physical responses to perceived threat:

When the Body Stiffens Involuntarily, It Is Revealing an Underlying Urge to Pull Away

One of the first signs that someone feels threatened is contraction — the body physically pulling inward.

Shoulders tense. Arms cross. Jaw clenches. The spine compresses. It may look like stress, but underneath, it signals:

"I want to disappear — or at least defend myself."

What it looks like:

- Shoulder hunching, as if bracing for impact
- Hands balling into fists or crossing over the stomach
- Neck slightly withdrawn into the shoulders
- Lips pressed or the jaw locked tight
- Chest no longer open — it "collapses" inward

This physical tightening is the body's attempt to:

- **Shrink target surface** (evolutionarily — make yourself smaller)
- **Protect vital organs** (heart, lungs, abdomen)
- **Prepare for withdrawal or silence**

It's not anger. It's not coldness. It's the body preparing to retreat from harm.

In high-stress environments — like tense conversations, confrontations, or high-stakes performance settings — you'll often see this full-body tightening, especially in people who are conflict-avoidant or emotionally overwhelmed.

Legs Pressed Together — a Subtle Sign of Avoidance

Our legs don't lie. In body language, the lower body often reveals **what the upper body tries to hide**. And one of the quietest signs of discomfort or internal defense is the **tight pressing of the legs together**, often seated but also standing.

What it signals:

- **Psychological self-protection**
- **Unconscious fear of judgment, rejection, or attack**
- **Readiness to withdraw without confrontation**

It's common in:

- Socially anxious individuals
- People on the receiving end of criticism or unwanted attention
- Situations involving emotional exposure, shame, or disapproval

Body language combinations:

- Hands in lap + legs crossed tightly = **retreat posture**
- Knees turned slightly away from others = **emotional disengagement**
- Feet angled inward = **lack of groundedness or confidence**

The legs don't just carry us — they signal whether we want to stay, run, or hide.

This leg tension may seem insignificant, but it often precedes more visible withdrawal — such as going silent, avoiding eye contact, or physically leaving the conversation.

Tiny Step Back:
The Subconscious Urge to Retreat

Sometimes, the body doesn't just tighten — it **moves**. But not with grand gestures. In threatening moments, people often take a **tiny step backward** — often imperceptible, but deeply revealing.

What it means:

- The person's brain has scanned the environment and said: *"Back away — this isn't safe."*

This happens when:

- Someone feels emotionally attacked or confronted
- A conversation becomes too intense or personal
- They're caught off guard by a boundary violation

It's especially noticeable during:

- Arguments
- Job interviews or high-stakes conversations
- Romantic vulnerability
- Social rejection or mockery

This micro-retreat isn't just social awkwardness. It's the **fight-or-flight** response activating quietly.

> *The body's saying: "I don't want to be in this moment."*

And here's the catch: most people don't realize they've done it. That **half-step back**, that **shift in weight**, or that slight increase in space — it's reflexive, and it's ancient.

Why the Body Speaks Before the Brain

These threat responses come from the **limbic system**, the emotional brain. It's fast, primitive, and designed for survival — not logic.

When we feel threatened:

- **The amygdala** detects danger (real or perceived)
- It signals the **autonomic nervous system** to activate
- The body tenses, breath shortens, and movements shift

And all of this happens before our conscious mind has time to say:

> *"Wait, maybe this isn't a real threat."*

Emotional threats that trigger this system:

- Fear of rejection
- Fear of failure
- Fear of humiliation
- Fear of conflict
- Fear of exposure or vulnerability

The modern world doesn't often threaten our physical safety — but our **emotional safety** is constantly on the line. And the body still reacts as if we're under attack.

Misreading These Signals Can Lead to Miscommunication

Imagine this:

- You're sharing your honest feelings with someone.
- They fold their arms. Their shoulders lift. Their legs press tight.
- They take a half-step back.

It's easy to think:

- *"They don't care."*
- *"They're shutting me out."*
- *"They're being cold or dismissive."*

But often, the reality is:

- **They're overwhelmed**, not disengaged
- **They're afraid**, not indifferent
- **They're processing**, not rejecting

That's the risk of ignoring body language — we interpret **protection as rejection**, and **discomfort as disinterest**.

How to Respond to Threat Reactions — In Others and Yourself

If you see these signs in someone else:

- **Lower your intensity** — soften voice, remove pressure
- **Acknowledge their discomfort** without judgment
  "I know this is a lot. You don't have to respond right away."
- **Give space** — physical and emotional
- **Avoid forcing eye contact or confrontation**

If you notice them in yourself:

- **Name the sensation**: "I'm tightening up — I must feel threatened."
- **Breathe deeply** — lengthen exhale to signal safety
- **Uncross your arms or legs** deliberately
- **Ground your feet** — feel connected to the present
- **Don't shame the reaction** — it's protective, not pathetic

Your body is not betraying you. It's trying to protect you — just in an outdated language.

Final Thought:
The Body Knows Before You Speak

We like to think communication is verbal. But often, the most honest part of us **doesn't use words.**

When someone tightens their body, presses their legs together, or takes a tiny step back — don't ignore it. Don't rush it. Don't shame it.

Instead, listen with your whole attention. Because in that tension is something deeply human:

> *A story of fear. A longing for safety. A request to be met with care.*

And when we meet that unspoken language with understanding, we give others — and ourselves — permission to feel safe enough to stay.

How the Body Reacts to Negative Judgments

Long before we defend ourselves with words, our body has already answered: "That hurt."

We are social beings, wired to seek belonging and avoid rejection. So when someone judges us harshly — whether it's a subtle remark or open criticism — the impact is not just emotional or mental.

It's physical.

The body feels the blow before the brain can rationalize it. Muscles shift. Posture collapses. Micro-reactions flicker across the face and limbs. These are not weaknesses. They are evolutionary reflexes — the body's attempt to protect the self in the face of perceived social threat.

Let's explore three key physical responses that reveal how the body internalizes and responds to negative judgment:

Drooping Shoulders: Hurt by Criticism

One of the most visible signs of feeling judged, rejected, or shamed is shoulder collapse. It's as if the weight of someone's words physically pulls the body downward.When someone hears criticism, their shoulders don't just fall — they fold in as if protecting the heart.

What it looks like:

- Shoulders slumping forward
- Neck slightly bowed
- Chest drawn inward
- Head lowered or chin tucked

This posture is a signal of:

- Emotional defeat
- Internal withdrawal
- Loss of perceived status or value

Even if the person doesn't respond verbally, their body might say:

"I heard that. And it hurt more than I want to admit."

Why it happens:

This reaction traces back to social hierarchy dynamics. In both human and animal behavior, lowering the body — especially the shoulders and head — is a sign of submission or retreat after disapproval.

It sends a message:

- "I yield"
- "I don't want to fight"
- "Please stop hurting me"

People with high sensitivity to feedback, social anxiety, or childhood experiences of harsh judgment often show this posture more intensely and frequently.

Shifting Gaze: Desire to Escape from becoming talk focus.

The eyes are not just windows to the soul — they're windows out. And when those windows suddenly shift, dart, or look away, it often means the person wants to exit the moment, psychologically or socially.

After judgment, you may see:

- Eye contact break instantly
- Gaze drop to the floor
- Looking to the side or at neutral objects (hands, walls, phone)
- Blink rate increase slightly

If someone blinks a lot around you, they are judging you.

The person isn't looking at you — they're looking for a way out. This is not always conscious. People don't usually decide to look away. The body just does it — in an attempt to:

- Reduce emotional intensity
- Avoid further exposure or scrutiny
- Find psychological safety away from the perceived threat

Culturally nuanced:

In some cultures, avoiding eye contact is a sign of respect. But in the context of criticism, shifting gaze almost always signals discomfort, insecurity, or emotional vulnerability.

You might notice:

- A confident person holds your gaze when challenged

- A self-conscious person glances away or preemptively looks down, expecting judgment

Face-Touching: A Sign of Self-Protection

Face-touching is one of the most frequent but overlooked nonverbal signals of discomfort. And it often spikes during moments of social threat, especially when someone feels judged.

Common behaviors:

- Rubbing the forehead
- Touching the mouth or chin
- Scratching the nose or cheek
- Covering part of the face with the hand

Touching the face is like the body trying to "cover" what feels exposed. What it communicates:

- Nervousness
- Shame
- An attempt to self-soothe
- A desire to hide, even slightly

From a psychological standpoint, the face is one of our most vulnerable areas. It displays emotion involuntarily — so when we feel judged, we try to regain control by touching or covering it.

Why it matters:
Face-touching after criticism may seem like a small habit, but in clusters with other behaviors — like slumped posture and gaze avoidance — it clearly shows emotional discomfort.

And sometimes, it reveals internal conflict:
"I want to defend myself, but I also don't want to make things worse."
"I don't know what to say, so I'll just hide a little until this passes."

The Deeper Psychology Behind These Reactions

The Brain Reads Judgment as Danger
When someone criticizes or disapproves of us, the amygdala (the brain's fear center) treats it as a social threat — not unlike physical danger.
It triggers:

- The fight-flight-freeze system
- Muscle tension, posture change, eye movement
- A shift away from connection, toward protection

Shame Is a Physical Emotion
Unlike guilt (which is mental and behavioral), shame lives in

the body. It causes people to shrink, lower their gaze, and want to disappear.

All three behaviors — shoulder drooping, gaze shifting, face-touching — are classic shame signals.

Shame doesn't yell. It folds inward, goes silent, and hides.

Social Hierarchy and Self-Worth
Humans are wired to maintain social belonging. Being judged threatens that belonging. The body reacts as if we're losing status or being cast out of the group.
That's why even subtle judgment — a sarcastic tone, an eye-roll, a pointed pause — can trigger strong physical reactions.

Misinterpretation: The Silent Damage

These subtle physical signs often go unnoticed or misread:

- A drooped posture may be seen as laziness
- Gaze avoidance may be mistaken for dishonesty
- Face-touching may be judged as nervous incompetence

But in reality, these are often the traces of social pain. And if we ignore them, we risk:

- Escalating conflict
- Shaming someone further
- Missing the opportunity to repair emotional safety

What You Can Do — For Others and Yourself

When you notice these signs in others:

- Lower your emotional intensity
  "I may have been too harsh — let's talk about it."
- Acknowledge vulnerability, not just behavior
  "I see this hit you harder than I thought. Can we pause?"
- Offer safe space to respond
  "Take your time — I'm listening, not judging."

When you feel them in yourself:

"Why did my shoulders just drop?"

"Why can't I look them in the eye?"

"Why am I touching my face right now?"

These questions aren't self-judgment — they're self-awareness. And once you recognize the body's alarm, you can:

- Breathe deeply
- Re-straighten your posture
- Reground in the present

Ask for a pause or space if needed
Self-compassion is the antidote to judgment — both from others, and from within.

Final Thought:
The Body Is Honest, Even When We Are Not

When someone feels judged, their body tells the truth.

- Their shoulders sink.
- Their eyes drift.
- Their hand covers the pain their words can't name.

Don't take these as signs of weakness. Take them as signals of impact.
Because when you notice what a body is trying to say — you may find what the person still can't say out loud:

"That hurt me. And I'm trying to hold myself together while I feel it."

Defeat Responses: What the Body Reveals

When words fail, the body confesses: "I've lost something."

Failure is universal — yet it rarely looks the same. Some people collapse into silence. Others explode in frustration. Many seem calm on the outside, while their body is screaming under the surface.

Defeat is not just a mental state — it's a **full-body experience**. And if you learn to read it, you'll see that the body offers **three distinct confessionals**: quiet withdrawal, visible frustration, and micro-emotional flickers that reveal the struggle to hold composure.

Let's break down the key body language cues of someone processing **defeat** — whether in an argument, a job interview, a performance, or a private failure.

Head Down and Silent: A Collapse of Ego?

When someone feels defeated, one of the first instinctive responses is to lower the head — paired with silence.

It's a movement so universal it appears in nearly every culture, sport, and species. Whether it's a student after a failed test, a boxer who lost a match, or a child being scolded, the posture says the same thing:

> *"I'm not proud right now."*
> *"I don't want to be seen."*

What it looks like:

- Chin tucked close to chest
- Eyes downcast or closed
- Shoulders slightly rounded
- Mouth shut, jaw slightly tense
- Lack of verbal participation

What it reveals:

- **Internal shame or self-directed anger**
- **A desire to reduce presence and attention**

- An emotional withdrawal to preserve dignity

This is more than just sadness — it's the **ego retreating.** When we feel judged, rejected, or like we've let ourselves down, the head-drop is a physical signal of surrender.

Psychologically, this posture reflects:

- **Collapse of perceived competence**
- Desire to **hide from the social spotlight**
- Activation of the **dorsal vagal nervous system**, which governs shut-down and withdrawal responses

The silence isn't emptiness. It's emotional overload. And the lowered head is not apathy — it's self-protection.

Face-Rubbing and Head-Grabbing: Frustration by Failure

While some people retreat inward during defeat, others go into **self-contact motion** — a kind of visible frustration loop.

These gestures are not random. They are unconscious attempts to **process intense emotional energy**, redirect internal heat, and — in some cases — **delay emotional expression** (like crying or shouting).

Common examples:

- Rubbing both hands over the face
- Dragging fingers through the hair
- Clutching the top or back of the head
- Palming the forehead
- Pressing both palms into the eyes

These are not just habits. They're emotional discharges — the body's way of saying: "This is too much."

What it communicates:

- **Self-directed frustration** ("Why did I do that?")
- **Mental chaos or emotional overload**
- **A desperate attempt to re-regulate or regroup**

These motions often occur:

- Immediately after making a mistake
- Upon hearing bad news or criticism
- When one's efforts have been rejected or invalidated

It's not unusual to see face-rubbing paired with sighs, muttered phrases ("Damn it"), or pacing. Together, they create a **nonverbal storm**: movement compensating for what words can't yet hold.

Rapid Blinking: Fighting Off Disappointment

Blinking may seem like a small detail — but it's a powerful emotional tell. When someone blinks rapidly after hearing bad news or experiencing a blow to their pride, they're not just "adjusting their eyes." They're **trying to regain emotional control.**

Why blinking speeds up:

- The nervous system becomes overstimulated
- Tear ducts activate slightly (even if the person doesn't cry)
- The brain is trying to stay present while the heart wants to **retreat**
- *Rapid blinking is a tension between composure and collapse.*

What it signals:

- **Emotional suppression** — holding back tears or a reaction
- **Internal conflict** — mind racing to find an explanation
- **Unspoken disappointment** — the kind that isn't safe (or ready) to express

Often, blinking is paired with:

- A tight jaw
- Quickened breathing
- Head slightly turned or eyes cast upward
- Fidgeting fingers or clenched hands

These small motions are the emotional equivalent of **white-knuckling through pain.** The person may appear "fine" — but their body is revealing the effort it takes to hold it together.

What Defeat Really Looks Like

Defeat doesn't always involve crying, yelling, or dramatic outbursts. It often shows up in:

- A quiet slump
- A hand to the face
- A blink that happens just a little too fast

These are **micro-failures of composure**, and they matter because they reveal the **truth beneath performance**. While someone might say "It's okay," their body says, "That stung."

Additional defeat cues:

- Slow exhale through the mouth (relief mixed with resignation)
- Sudden drop in energy or animation
- Losing eye contact completely
- Resting the head in hands for extended moments

In group settings — like meetings or social conflicts — these signs often go unnoticed. But for emotionally attuned observers, they're signals to **pause, de-escalate, or offer space.**

The Science Behind It: Why the Body Surrenders First

Our bodies evolved to register failure as threat — especially social failure.

In tribal life, being rejected or criticized could mean losing status, protection, or even survival. So the **limbic brain** (particularly the amygdala and anterior cingulate cortex) reacts to social defeat **like physical pain.**

This results in:

- Muscle tension or collapse
- Nervous tics (face-touching, blinking, rocking)

- Shutdown of verbal regions (leading to silence)

The body goes offline, or into overdrive — long before the person can explain what they're feeling.

How to Support Someone Processing Defeat

You don't need the perfect words. You just need to **recognize the signals** and offer **relief from further judgment.**

Try this:

- **Respect the silence** — don't rush them to speak
- **Acknowledge the moment**
  "I know this was hard."
- **Offer nonverbal grounding** — water, presence, calmness
- **Don't interpret frustration as aggression**
  Face-rubbing doesn't mean "angry at you" — it often means "angry at self"

Compassion doesn't require answers — only presence.

Final Thought:
The Body Grieves the Loss of Pride

Defeat isn't always loud. Sometimes it's a quiet slump. Sometimes it's hands covering a face. Sometimes it's blinking faster than usual in a room that suddenly feels too bright.

If you learn to see these cues, you'll begin to understand people at their most vulnerable — the moment when their pride breaks, and their humanity is most visible.

Because in that moment, whether through slumped shoulders or a single blink, the body isn't just reacting.

It's asking:

> *"Will you still respect me, even now?"*

Physical Signs of Insecurity

Insecurity doesn't always speak. Sometimes it folds its arms, shrinks its neck, and shuffles its feet.

Insecurity isn't always loud or obvious. Often, it hides beneath the surface — in posture, movement, and subtle cues that reveal discomfort before a single word is spoken.

Whether it stems from social anxiety, low self-worth, or fear of rejection, **the body often betrays what the mind tries to conceal**. By recognizing these physical signs, we not only better understand others, but also grow more compassionate toward our own internal struggles.

Let's explore three common and powerful body language signals that often indicate **insecurity in action**:

Crossed Arms: Building a Psychological Wall

One of the most recognizable — and misunderstood — body language signals is the crossing of arms.

People often interpret it as a sign of stubbornness, coldness, or defiance. But in many cases, **crossed arms reflect insecurity**, not hostility.

When the world feels threatening, the body builds a barrier.

What it looks like:

- Arms crossed tightly over the chest
- Hands gripping opposite arms or tucking into armpits
- Shoulders slightly hunched inward
- Posture becomes smaller or less open

What it communicates:

- **Emotional self-protection**
- **Fear of exposure**
- **Attempt to comfort oneself subconsciously**

From a psychological perspective, this posture:

- **Creates a sense of boundary** when one doesn't feel safe
- Reduces vulnerability by protecting the torso — where the heart and lungs are
- Provides tactile feedback (the pressure of one's own arms) that can be calming under stress

You'll often see this in:

- Group settings when someone feels like an outsider
- Conversations where criticism or judgment is expected
- People who struggle with confidence or social anxiety

It's not that they don't want to connect — it's that they don't feel safe enough to.

Shrinking the Neck: Avoid Exposing Vulnerability

When people feel insecure or threatened — even emotionally — they often engage in an unconscious gesture: **pulling their neck inward**, almost as if trying to hide inside themselves.

It's subtle, but powerful. And it reveals a deep desire to become **smaller, safer, less seen.**

How it shows up:

- Shoulders lift slightly
- Neck retracts (head sits lower than usual)
- Chin tilts downward, sometimes tucked toward the chest
- Facial expression appears tentative, uncertain, or wary

It's a turtle response: when the world feels sharp, the neck retreats.

This movement is part of a broader "**withdrawal posture**", often seen in:

- Students when asked a question they're unsure of
- Employees receiving unexpected critique
- Anyone afraid of saying the wrong thing or being judged for how they look or sound

Psychological function:

- Protects the throat — one of the body's vulnerable zones
- Reduces eye-level engagement (and therefore social threat)
- Symbolically shrinks the body to appear less threatening — or less threatened

This gesture may look passive, but it's **full of emotional noise.** It reflects the person's inward collapse, the mind saying:

> *"If I could disappear right now, I would."*

Shuffling Feet: A Restless Mind Made Visible

While crossed arms and a tucked neck reflect **protective stillness**, shuffling feet reveal **internal restlessness** — the nervous energy of someone caught in self-doubt, discomfort, or uncertainty.

What it looks like:

- Shifting weight from one foot to the other
- Sliding or dragging feet slightly without walking
- Toes pointing inward or constantly repositioning
- Feet tapping or fidgeting subtly beneath the table

When the mind doesn't feel grounded, neither do the feet.

This is especially common in:

- Social situations with strangers
- Public speaking or presentation settings

- Moments of waiting for judgment or evaluation

While the **upper body may remain composed**, the feet often tell the truth. They show the person is:

- **Debating whether to stay or go**
- **Searching for stability** in an emotionally shaky situation
- **Trying to release nervous energy** without drawing attention

Neurological basis:

The brain detects discomfort → increases adrenaline → causes **micro-movements** in the legs and feet. Even if the person wants to appear calm, their **limbic system** is still preparing for flight.

That's why therapists, interviewers, and even interrogators often watch the **feet first**, not the face — because the **feet rarely lie**.

Why Insecurity Shows Up in the Body

Insecurity is not just a thought — it's a **felt sense of internal instability**. And when the mind feels unsafe, the body responds in three key ways:

- **Protection** — arms cross, chest hides, boundaries go up
- **Contraction** — neck shrinks, shoulders rise, posture collapses

- **Escape drive** — feet move, eyes shift, the body prepares to leave

These responses come from the **autonomic nervous system**, especially the **sympathetic branch** (fight-or-flight) and **dorsal vagal response** (freeze or shut down).

The insecure body is not malfunctioning. It's defending.

Whether the perceived threat is social (judgment), emotional (rejection), or physical (being watched), the body doesn't wait for logic. It reacts.

What We Often Get Wrong About Insecurity

People frequently misread these physical signals:

- **Crossed arms** are seen as being cold or arrogant — instead of scared.
- **Tucked necks** are viewed as disinterest — instead of self-protection.
- **Fidgety feet** are interpreted as impatience — rather than anxiety.

This leads to misunderstandings, hurtful assumptions, and missed opportunities for empathy.

But once you understand the **body's insecurity code**, you start seeing people differently — not as "closed off," but as **yearning for psychological safety**.

How to Respond — With Others and Yourself

When you notice these signs in someone else:

- **Don't confront it directly** (e.g., "Why are you fidgeting?") — this can deepen insecurity
- **Create space** by lowering intensity, softening tone, giving time
- **Reassure subtly:**
  "No pressure."
  "We're just talking, no judgment."
  "Take your time — you're doing fine."

When you notice them in yourself:

- Name it: "*My arms are crossed — I must feel exposed.*"
- Breathe into the discomfort: long exhale = safety signal to the brain
- Deliberately **uncross, lift, and ground:** posture adjustment can shift inner state
- Remember: **Insecurity is not a flaw. It's a signal.** It means your mind is working hard to stay safe in a moment that feels uncertain.

The goal is not to eliminate insecurity. It's to meet it without judgment — in others and in ourselves.

Final Thought: Insecurity Is the Body Whispering, "Please Be Gentle With Me"

Crossed arms don't always mean defiance. Shrunk necks aren't about disinterest. Shuffling feet aren't a sign of boredom.

All three are **emotional shields**. And behind those shields is usually someone saying:

> *"I want to be here... but I'm afraid of what you'll think of me."*

When you learn to read these signs — and respond with calm, warmth, and presence — you help turn insecurity into something powerful:

> Not a weakness to fix,
>
> But **a moment of humanity to respect.**

Chapter 6

Recognizing Personality Types Through Behavior

Traits of People Who Talk Behind Your Back

They smile to your face, but their body tells another story.

Few social behaviors are more damaging — or more common — than talking behind someone's back. It erodes trust, fractures relationships, and creates invisible tension in personal and professional environments. But here's the challenge: **most people won't tell you they're doing it.** In fact, many go to great lengths to appear friendly in person — all while undermining you in private.

But behavior rarely lies. People who talk behind your back often display subtle but consistent **nonverbal cues** that reveal their discomfort, guilt, or two-faced intent. Their bodies can't fully hide what their words try to conceal.

This article explores three key behavioral traits commonly seen in those who **speak ill of others behind closed doors,** but act polite to their faces:

They Lower Their Heads When They Say Bad Things

One of the most overlooked signals of backstabbing behavior is a **downward tilt of the head**, especially when someone is gossiping, criticizing, or spreading rumors.

This action is rarely conscious. It's a subtle body language cue associated with **shame, secrecy, or avoidance.** When someone lowers their head while speaking negatively — especially in hushed tones or private settings — it's often because **they know they're doing something socially risky.**

Why it happens:

- Lowering the head is a **submissive gesture**, signaling discomfort or lack of confidence in one's actions
- It's also a **way of hiding** — minimizing exposure, like animals who lower their gaze when feeling guilty or cornered
- In gossip situations, it serves as a **physical attempt to escape accountability**

You might observe this behavior:

- When someone leans in to whisper something negative, but looks down as they say it
- When they talk poorly about someone, but avoid looking around the room (as if scanning for danger)

- When they immediately shift to "smiling mode" if the person they were talking about enters the space

Lowered heads often carry heavy words.

This behavior is most common in people who:

- Don't like confrontation but still need to vent
- Feel jealous or threatened by someone but lack the courage to express it directly
- Seek validation from others by tearing someone else down

They Can't Hold Eye Contact When They See You

Here's the contradiction: someone talks about you when you're not around, but pretends everything's fine when you are. The human mind can try to pull off this double act — but the eyes often expose the truth.

When someone has spoken negatively about you behind your back, **maintaining normal eye contact** with you becomes psychologically difficult. Why? Because looking someone in the eyes while holding a secret or internal judgment creates emotional friction.

Common signs:

- Their gaze **flickers away quickly** when you start speaking
- They look at your forehead, mouth, or somewhere over your shoulder
- They may blink more than usual or touch their face while talking to you
- In group settings, they avoid standing or sitting directly across from you

Why it matters:

Eye contact is deeply tied to **trust, openness, and congruence.** When those things are missing — especially due to guilt, anxiety, or resentment — people instinctively **break the gaze.** This is especially true when the person they're facing is the **subject of their recent gossip.**

> *Avoiding eye contact is the body's way of saying: "I can't face the truth — or you."*

Note: some people naturally avoid eye contact due to social anxiety or cultural norms, so it's important to **observe changes** in their behavior. If someone used to maintain strong eye contact with you, but now frequently looks away or seems visually uncomfortable — especially after a conflict or success on your part — it could be a red flag.

They Have Closed Lips When Speaking to You

The lips are one of the most **expressive parts of the body**, especially when people are trying not to say something. One of the most telling cues of inner conflict, suppression, or unspoken negativity is **pressed lips** — where the lips are held tightly together in a straight line.

What it means:

Pressed lips signal **withholding** — not just information, but emotion. It's often a physical manifestation of thoughts like:

- *"I don't want to reveal what I'm really thinking."*
- *"I've said something behind your back, and now I have to be careful not to slip."*
- *"I disapprove of you, but I'll keep it polite — for now."*

In conversation, pressed lips may appear:

- As a quick flash when someone is **asked a direct question**
- During pauses where they could offer praise or support, but don't
- Right before they change the subject to avoid emotional discomfort

The key here is **contrast**. If someone smiles and chats with others freely, but becomes noticeably **tight-lipped and neutral** when talking to you, it may suggest they feel internally conflicted.

Smiles fade. But the tension in the lips often lingers.

This sign is especially revealing in one-on-one interactions, where **politeness is maintained but warmth is missing**. The person may nod, offer surface-level responses, and even say the "right" things — but their lips remain firm, unyielding. They're guarding something.

The Psychology of Talking Behind Someone's Back

Why do people gossip or speak badly of others in secret — but act kind in person?
At the root of this behavior are **three psychological drivers:**

1. Cowardice

Some people want to express their opinions but **lack the courage** to do so directly. So they turn to third parties, hoping to be validated without taking interpersonal risk.

2. Envy

Talking behind someone's back can be a symptom of **envy masked as critique.** Instead of admitting they feel threatened or "less than," the person reshapes the story:
"They don't really deserve what they have."

3. Social Manipulation

Some individuals use gossip to **build alliances**. By speaking ill of someone, they attempt to draw others closer — bonding through shared negativity or positioning themselves as "truth-tellers."

They don't always hate you. But they hate the way you make them feel about themselves.

How to Handle It

If you suspect someone is talking behind your back:

- **Observe patterns** — don't rely on single moments. Look for consistent avoidance, coldness, or indirect tension
- **Protect your energy** — don't chase approval. Maintain your integrity
- **Confront only if necessary**, and do it from a place of clarity, not accusation:

"I've sensed some tension lately — is there something I should know?"

If you catch yourself doing it:

- Ask: Why can't I say this directly? What fear is stopping me?
- Practice speaking **with honesty, but without harm**
- Remember: talking behind others' backs may give short-term relief, but it creates **long-term disconnection**

Final Reflection: Secrets Leave Shadows

People may try to hide their betrayal behind smiles, compliments, or polite greetings. But their bodies — their lowered gaze, their lips, their eyes — **often reveal the truth.**

> *You can fake your words. You can even fake your smile. But your nervous system doesn't lie.*

Learning to read these signals isn't about becoming paranoid — it's about becoming aware. Not everyone who lowers their eyes is dishonest. Not everyone who presses their lips is hiding something.

But when the behavior matches the intuition, and the vibe shifts subtly but clearly — it's worth paying attention.

Because in the world of human behavior, **truth is rarely loud — but it is visible.**

Signs That Someone Doesn' t Like You

They may not say it, but their silence — and posture — speak louder than words.

Dislike is a feeling most people won't express openly. Whether due to social politeness, workplace politics, or personal avoidance, people often mask their true feelings. But here's the truth: while words can lie, **the body rarely does.**

The human nervous system reacts faster than conscious thought. Subtle gestures, expressions, and energy shifts can reveal someone's **true emotional stance**, even if their mouth says, "*No, everything's fine.*"

In this article, we explore three of the most reliable **nonverbal signs that someone doesn't like you:**

- They avoid eye contact
- They give minimal responses
- They physically turn away

Let's break them down, one by one.

Avoiding Eye Contact: A Sign of Disinterest

Eye contact is fundamental to human connection. It signals presence, interest, and emotional openness. When someone avoids making or holding eye contact with you — and only you — that's often a clear indication of **discomfort or disinterest.**

What it looks like:

They quickly glance away when you look at them

They focus on their phone, surroundings, or others in the room

When speaking, they direct their attention toward the floor or away from your face

Their gaze feels scattered or half-present

Avoiding eye contact can mean different things in different contexts — social anxiety, cultural norms, or shyness. But when someone **used to make eye contact** and then suddenly stops — or when they engage with others but **not you** — it's often personal.

> *"The eyes avoid what the heart wants to reject."*

Why it matters:

Avoiding eye contact minimizes emotional connection. It sends a subconscious message:

"I don't want to connect with you. I don't want to be seen by you."

In romantic contexts, this can signal fading attraction. In friendships, it often means **distance or distrust**. In professional settings, it could suggest **resentment, competition, or low regard.**

Minimal Responses Signal Hidden Disapproval

When someone doesn't like you, they rarely say it directly. Instead, they often use **verbal detachment**: short, empty responses that keep the interaction technically polite, but emotionally cold.

What it sounds like:

"Yeah."

"Okay."

"Cool."

"That's nice."

You might notice:

- No questions or follow-ups
- No warmth in tone

No laughter, enthusiasm, or mirroring of your mood

A sense that you're **talking "at" them**, not with them

Even when you share something meaningful — a success, a struggle, or a joke — their response is underwhelming, as if they're **checking a social box** rather than truly engaging.

They're present, but not participating.

This kind of minimalism often arises from **dislike mixed with suppression**. They may not feel free to express disapproval directly, so they withdraw instead.

Why it matters:

Words become emotionally flat when people feel:

- Disconnected from you
- Judgmental or critical but unwilling to show it
- Bored or irritated by your presence

This is especially telling when their communication style **differs with others**. If they're chatty with some, but emotionally distant with you — it's likely not accidental.

Turning Away: The Body's Way of Saying "No"

In psychology, the direction someone's body faces is a powerful indicator of **affiliation**. We unconsciously **orient ourselves toward people we feel connected to** — and away from those we want to avoid.

What it looks like:

- Their torso, feet, or legs **face away** from you in a group
- They sit or stand at an angle that closes off interaction
- They lean **out of** conversations, not in
- Objects (like bags or coffee cups) are subtly used as **barriers** between you

Turning away is rarely aggressive — but it's very clear. It's the body's way of creating distance without words.

> *"Where the body points, the heart follows."*

This behavior becomes more noticeable when:

- The person doesn't adjust their body even when you speak directly to them
- They look "ready to leave" or "on their way out" of the interaction
- They literally take steps back or reposition themselves when you approach

Why it matters:

Turning away reflects a subconscious desire to:

- Exit the interaction
- Reduce emotional exposure
- Signal disengagement without confrontation

In relationships of all kinds, physical turning away is often the **first sign of a deeper emotional turn.**

Other Red Flags That Reinforce the Signs

These three behaviors are the foundation, but here are a few **bonus indicators** to watch for when suspecting someone doesn't like you:

- **Delayed or one-sided texting**: dry, short, and non-curious replies
- **No social curiosity**: they don't ask about your life, ideas, or emotions
- **Micro-expressions of contempt**: slight sneers, nose wrinkles, or eye rolls
- **Social exclusion**: they subtly avoid sitting next to you, inviting you, or including you
- **Fake politeness**: exaggerated smiles with cold undertones

It's the pattern that matters, not any one sign. People have off days. But if you're noticing all three signs — plus the above — across multiple interactions, it's worth trusting your gut.

Why They Won't Just Tell You

If someone doesn't like you, why don't they just say so?

1. Social Conditioning
Politeness is rewarded. Confrontation is uncomfortable. Many people are taught never to express dislike directly — so they avoid, withdraw, and suppress.

2. Power Dynamics
In workplaces or group settings, people fear the consequences of conflict. They hide behind smiles to avoid escalation.

3. Insecurity
Some people **want to be liked** even by those they dislike. So instead of being honest, they act neutral — while secretly resenting the interaction.

Ironically, some of the people who dislike you most will act **overly friendly** — not because they care, but because they want to **hide their feelings**, or even manipulate impressions.

What to Do If You Suspect It's Happening

1. Observe, Don't Obsess
It's not about becoming paranoid. Watch patterns. Take note. Then ask yourself: Does this connection feel mutual?

2. Pull Back Your Emotional Investment

You don't owe energy to someone who's clearly checked out. You deserve to be in relationships — personal or professional — where warmth flows both ways.

3. Stay Kind, but Clear

Dislike doesn't need to be met with defensiveness. Often, your maturity and clarity will speak louder than their passive discomfort.

You don't have to prove your worth to someone who's already looking away.

Final Thought: Emotional Honesty Is in the Body

Not everyone will tell you the truth with their words. But their posture will.Their eyes will.Their tone, their presence, and their subtle shifts — they all form a quiet language.

If you feel dismissed, minimized, or frozen out, trust what your nervous system is picking up.

And remember:

When someone's body says "no," don't beg for a "yes."

The right people will face you, look you in the eyes, and respond with full hearts. Let the rest fall away.

How to Recognize a Dominant Personality

Control isn't always loud. But with dominant people, it often walks fast, talks louder, and takes the lead without asking.

Dominance is one of the most observable personality traits — yet it rarely calls itself by name. Dominant individuals don't always tell you they want control; instead, they move through the world in a way that assumes it's already theirs.

Whether in relationships, work, or social settings, dominant personalities tend to assert influence without invitation. They rarely ask for permission, and they often don't wait for consensus.

So how can you spot a dominant person early? You look at what they do — not just what they say.
Here are three reliable behavioral clues to recognize a dominant personality in action:

Fast Walkers, Loud Talkers: Micro-Traces of Control

One of the most overlooked signs of dominance lies in the pace and volume of basic behaviors — walking and talking.

Dominant people often walk quickly and purposefully, especially in shared environments. Their movements are direct, unhesitant, and rarely follow others. If in a group, they often walk ahead or dictate the pace — as if others should catch up. Likewise, their speech is typically:

- Louder than average, even in quiet rooms
- Marked by projected volume that fills space confidently
- Delivered with minimal hesitation, few filler words, and strong intonation

The dominant person's body says: "I know where I'm going." Their voice says: "You should listen."

Why it matters:

Walking fast signals internal urgency, control, and decisiveness.

Speaking loudly is not always aggression — it's often a claim to social space.

Both together form an energetic dominance: the sense that this person takes up room, moves through life first, and doesn't ask for permission.

These behaviors are usually habitual, not performative. Dominant individuals often don't even realize they're walking ahead or interrupting — because in their world, that's simply how things work.

Always Leading the Conversation, Rarely Yielding

In conversations, dominant personalities take on the role of director — sometimes subtly, sometimes aggressively. They often:

- Initiate the topic
- Control the rhythm and turn-taking
- Shift the subject quickly when bored
- Interrupt others when they feel the need to clarify or correct

While confident people may also speak up frequently, dominant people go one step further: they don't just participate — they structure the flow.

What it sounds like:

"Let me stop you there..."
"What you really mean is..."
"Here's the deal..."
"Anyway, what I was saying earlier..."

This often shows up in group dynamics, where the dominant person:

- Summarizes what others say (even without being asked)
- Speaks over quieter voices
- Feels entitled to the final word

Dominance in speech isn't just about talking — it's about steering.And when someone else leads the conversation? Dominant individuals may:

- Appear visibly impatient
- Look away or fidget
- Redirect the discussion back to themselves or what they deem "important"

This isn't necessarily rudeness — it's more often ego-led urgency. They believe their perspective brings clarity, and they're internally wired to take command of verbal space.

In Public, Their Dominance Intensifies

Interestingly, dominant individuals often amplify their behavior in public — especially in competitive or social environments.

In private, their control may be subtle: choosing where to sit, making final decisions, or setting expectations in relationships.
But in public, dominance becomes performative:

- Stronger voice projection in meetings or social events
- Body positioning that places them in central or higher-status spots (e.g., head of the table, standing while others sit)
- Interrupting or "owning the room" during conversations
- Offering unsolicited advice, critiques, or corrections — often to reinforce perceived hierarchy

Dominant people thrive in environments where status can be displayed, reinforced, or reclaimed.
They may also engage in status rituals:

- Name-dropping
- Mentioning achievements or credentials
- Telling stories that subtly establish superiority (e.g., "When I handled something like this at my last company...")

In romantic contexts, public dominance may show as:

- Taking control of logistics or planning without discussion
- Ordering for both people at restaurants
- Correcting or rephrasing their partner in front of others

These behaviors don't always stem from malice — often, they reflect a deep need to stay in charge of image, outcome, and attention.

What's Underneath Dominant Behavior?

It's tempting to label dominance as arrogance or control issues. But many dominant personalities are not malicious — they're driven.

Psychologically, dominance can stem from:

- High self-confidence
  They believe their decisions are right — and they want others to benefit from that certainty.

- Fear of vulnerability
  Taking control is often a defense against chaos. For some, dominance becomes a shield that hides emotional unpredictability.

- Early learned roles
  Some people were raised to lead, solve problems, or "take care of things." Their dominance is a script, not a scheme.

That said, unregulated dominance can become problematic:

- Others feel steamrolled or unimportant

- Emotional intimacy is blocked by control-as-connection

- Group dynamics suffer due to imbalanced participation

How to Respond to a Dominant Personality

If you're around one:

- Don't compete head-on, unless necessary. Instead, set clear boundaries and calmly claim space
- Use direct statements:
  "Let me finish my thought before we shift."
  "I'd like to bring someone else into the conversation."
- Use body positioning to reclaim nonverbal authority — face them squarely, match their energy

If you are one:

- Ask: Am I leading, or am I controlling?
- Make room for silence. Invite others to contribute. Wait before correcting
- Remember: collaboration doesn't weaken you — it amplifies you
- True power doesn't silence others — it brings out the best in them.

Final Thought:
Dominance Is a Volume, Not a Virtue

Dominant people aren't always bad. In fact, many make great leaders, decision-makers, and protectors. But the line between healthy confidence and ego-driven control is thin.

Recognizing a dominant personality isn't about labeling — it's about reading the room. Who speaks first? Who moves fast? Who needs to win small moments — even when no one else is playing?

The answers lie not in what they say, but in how they walk, how they speak, and how much space they believe they deserve — with or without your agreement.

A Story of Clever Dominance and Psychological Influence

To truly understand dominance beyond surface behavior, consider this story:
A clever businessman once purchased a large, abandoned piece of land with the intent to convert it into a vineyard. However, the local workers were notoriously lazy and unwilling to take on hard labor unless paid exorbitant wages. Faced with this challenge, the businessman devised a psychological strategy rather than a straightforward financial offer.

He secretly buried fake "gold nuggets" throughout the property, then acted as if he were angry and driving workers away, creating the illusion that the land contained valuable gold deposits. Word quickly spread through the small town that there was gold to be found. Soon, hundreds of people returned at night to dig and clear the land frantically, completing in three days what would have otherwise taken months of paid labor.

Later, these people were accused of trespassing and theft because they had entered the land without permission. Pressured and caught in the legal aftermath, many signed labor contracts agreeing to work for the businessman long-term.

Through this intricate psychological manipulation – using greed and the promise of wealth – the businessman not only cleared his land for free but also secured a reliable workforce. He became a local hero, while those who were tricked into working for him became his devoted followers, often unaware of how they had been subtly controlled.

This story vividly illustrates how dominance and influence go beyond words and overt commands. True dominance often operates behind the scenes, using psychological levers like motivation, perception, and social pressure to shape outcomes.

The same principles apply in everyday life: understanding the behaviors and subtle cues of dominant personalities can help you navigate complex social dynamics, identify when influence is being exerted, and use that knowledge wisely to maintain your own autonomy.

This book helps you understand others' words, tone, body language, and habits — how to recognize emotional levers and leverage them intelligently.

Behavioral Patterns of Overly Cautious People

They plan, hesitate, re-check, and sometimes miss out — not because they don't care, but because they care too much about what could go wrong.

Caution is a virtue — until it becomes a prison. While being careful can protect us from reckless decisions, **over-caution** often signals deeper emotional and cognitive patterns rooted in fear, control, or a history of disappointment.

Overly cautious people are not lazy, slow, or indecisive by nature. Rather, they've trained themselves — consciously or not — to think before they leap, double-check before they speak, and **avoid risk at nearly all costs.**

So how can you recognize an overly cautious personality in behavior? Look beyond their words, and observe these **consistent patterns of action and interaction:**

Delayed Decisions, Even on Small Matters

One of the most noticeable traits of overly cautious individuals is how long they take to **make even minor choices**. They'll hesitate between restaurant menus, reread email drafts multiple times, or delay purchases far longer than necessary.

What it looks like:

- Constantly comparing options ("Should I choose A, or maybe B... or wait for C?")
- Needing to "sleep on it" for almost every decision
- Seeking reassurance from others before moving forward
- Regret after choosing — not because the decision was wrong, but because it could have been better

Over-caution makes "deciding" feel like gambling.

Why it happens:

- Fear of making the **wrong choice**
- Deep need for **certainty and control**
- Internalized belief that mistakes are dangerous, not learning opportunities

This behavior can be frustrating in group settings, especially when tasks require momentum. But it often masks a deeply rooted fear of being **blamed, judged, or disappointed.**

Overthinking and Worst-Case Scenarios

Cautious people are **excellent analysts** — but their minds often spiral into **catastrophic thinking.**

They visualize what could go wrong in exquisite detail. They don't just see risk — they live it *in advance* through mental simulation.

Common signs:

- Rehearsing conversations before they happen
- Preparing multiple backup plans for unlikely situations
- Asking "What if..." questions in a loop
- Avoiding action because there's always one more thing to consider

Caution becomes a mental rehearsal for failure.

This hyper-vigilance can appear like being "meticulous" or "responsible," but underneath is a nervous system trained to **scan for danger**, not opportunity.

Such people often experience:

- **Decision fatigue**
- **Burnout from planning**
- **Analysis paralysis** — where thinking replaces doing

Reluctance to Try New or Unfamiliar Things

Overly cautious individuals tend to stay within known zones. Newness — whether people, places, or processes — introduces uncertainty, which they instinctively avoid.

Examples:

- Preferring routines over novelty
- Eating at the same restaurants, taking the same route, choosing the same brands
- Saying "maybe later" or "let me think about it" when invited to new experiences
- Avoiding tasks where there's a learning curve or risk of failure

"New" isn't exciting to them — it's threatening.

This caution around novelty often makes them appear:

- Inflexible or rigid
- Unadventurous
- Overly dependent on structure

But it's not about a lack of curiosity — it's about **self-protection**. Their nervous system interprets uncertainty as danger.

Excessive Need for Reassurance

Another key behavior: **asking for permission, validation, or backup** even when it's unnecessary.

Cautious people often seek out:

- "Does this make sense to you?"
- "What would you do in my situation?"
- "Do you think I'm overreacting?"

They're not fishing for compliments. They're scanning for **safety.** When someone else validates their thought process, it temporarily **soothes their fear of doing something wrong.**

This looks like:

- Checking in repeatedly with authority figures or peers
- Needing external opinions before moving forward
- Repeating their concerns even after reassurance has been given

They aren't indecisive — they're unsure they're "allowed" to decide.

Over time, this pattern may create **dependency** in relationships, where they rely on o thers to act as emotional "seatbelts."

Conflict Avoidance and Non-Confrontational Behavior

Cautious personalities usually hate conflict. They see arguments not as opportunities to resolve — but as risks of **emotional rupture.**

They often:

- Suppress their opinions to avoid upsetting others
- Say "yes" even when they mean "no"
- Apologize first, even when they're not at fault
- Avoid expressing boundaries clearly

In group dynamics, this may appear as **agreeableness**, but in reality it's **fear-based compliance.**

Peace is not always connection — sometimes it's avoidance wearing a polite smile.

This leads to:

- Bottled resentment
- Feeling misunderstood or unseen
- Passive-aggressive behavior when frustration eventually leaks out

Over-Preparedness in Daily Tasks

Many overly cautious individuals overcompensate for anxiety by **over-preparing**. They bring umbrellas even when it's sunny. They triple-check meeting times. They carry backup chargers, snacks, maps, and medications — just in case.

What it reflects:

- An attempt to **control external unpredictability**
- Subconscious fear that something will go wrong if they're not ready

Internal voice that says: "*If something happens, it's my fault for not planning.*"

This preparedness can make them **dependable** and **resourceful,** but also:

- Exhausted
- Rigid
- Anxious when plans go off-script

When you always prepare for the worst, it's hard to enjoy the best.

Where Does Over-Caution Come From ?

Over-cautious behavior isn't random. It often stems from:

1. Early Life Conditioning

Childhoods where mistakes were punished harshly — emotionally or physically — often teach people that **error = danger.** So they grow up over-correcting.

2. Anxious Temperament

Some people are wired with more **sensitive nervous systems**, causing them to be more reactive to uncertainty, noise, or social ambiguity.

3. Negative Experiences with Risk

If someone took a risk and was betrayed, embarrassed, or failed publicly, the brain stores that as a warning: "*Don't do that again.*"

How to Help — Or Self-Regulate

If you love or work with an overly cautious person:

Don't mock or rush them. That only amplifies their freeze response

Instead, gently **encourage small risks**, and celebrate them.
Provide emotional safety by saying things like:

> *"It's okay if it doesn't go perfectly — we'll figure it out."*

If you are one:

Remind yourself: **mistakes = growth, not shame**

Practice **low-stakes risks**: try something new each week

Set timers for decisions: "*I'll choose in 10 minutes, even if it's not perfect.*"

Use grounding mantras like:

> *"I can handle discomfort."*
> *"I don't need to be perfect to be safe."*

Final Thought:
Caution Is a Strategy, Not an Identity

Over-caution isn't a flaw — it's an adaptation. A strategy built over time to protect yourself from pain, chaos, or rejection.

But when that strategy starts costing you opportunity, spontaneity, and joy, it's time to loosen the grip.

You don't need to live like something might go wrong.
You can live like something good might happen.

Let caution be a tool — not a cage.

How Emotionally Immature People Behave

They may look like adults, but inside, their emotions are still trying to grow up.

Emotional immaturity has little to do with age. Some people grow older without ever developing the emotional regulation, self-awareness, or interpersonal responsibility that adulthood requires.

At first glance, emotionally immature people may seem normal—even likable. But over time, their behavioral patterns create chaos: in relationships, in communication, and especially in conflict.

They aren't "bad" people. But they are often **hard to connect with** on a healthy, stable, and reciprocal level. That's because emotional immaturity creates behaviors that avoid accountability, resist self-reflection, and protect the ego at all costs.

So how do emotionally immature people behave?
Here are three of the most common and revealing patterns:

Blaming Others Is Their Default Defense

Emotionally immature people struggle to take personal responsibility. When things go wrong — in work, relationships, or daily life — their first instinct is to point outward, not inward.

What it sounds like:

- *"If you hadn't said that, I wouldn't have reacted this way."*
- *"This wouldn't have happened if you just listened to me."*
- *"People are always trying to make me the bad guy."*

Instead of reflecting on their own role, emotionally immature people instinctively shift blame:

- Onto partners, colleagues, family members
- Onto circumstances ("I was just tired, okay?"
- Onto abstract forces (e.g., "The world is against me")

Blame becomes a shield — protecting them from the discomfort of being wrong.

Why they do it:

- Their self-image is fragile, so admitting fault feels threatening
- Accountability feels like punishment, not growth
- They may have grown up in environments where mistakes were met with shame, not learning

Over time, this behavior leads to:

- **Broken trust** in relationships
- **Frustrated communication** at work
- Emotional burnout for anyone close to them, especially partners or friends who are expected to "absorb" their blame

Emotional Rollercoaster: From Happy to Rage Instantly

Another hallmark of emotional immaturity is **emotional volatility** — big feelings that swing dramatically, with little regulation or self-awareness.

They may seem happy and loving one minute, then cold, sarcastic, angry, or withdrawn the next — with no clear explanation.

What it looks like:

- Overreacting to minor setbacks
- Shifting moods rapidly in response to small triggers
- Using emotional outbursts to manipulate or control conversations
- Turning a calm moment into an argument with very little provocation

Mature people manage emotions. Immature people become their emotions.

They often believe that:

- Their feelings **justify their behavior**, no matter how hurtful
- If they feel something strongly, then **others must cater to it**
- Expressing anger or sadness loudly will get them what they want

These patterns can make relationships feel like **walking on eggshells**. You never know what mood they'll bring — or what version of them you're going to get.

"That's Just Who I Am" Is an Emotional Escape Mechanism

Perhaps the most revealing sign of emotional immaturity is a person's **refusal to grow.**

Instead of acknowledging harmful behavior and working to change it, they hide behind rigid self-labels like:

- *"I'm just honest — people are too sensitive."*
- *"I don't do emotions, okay?"*
- *"I've always been like this. If you don't like it, leave."*

These statements are not expressions of identity — they're **excuses for not evolving.**

"That's just who I am" often means: "I don't want to take emotional responsibility."

Why it matters:

Mature individuals understand that growth is uncomfortable — but necessary.Immature individuals see any challenge to their behavior as a **personal attack**, not an invitation to reflect.

This leads to:

- **Stagnation in personal development**

- **Repeated patterns in relationships** (e.g., always pushing people away when conflict arises)
- A belief that **others must adapt** to their emotional immaturity, rather than the other way around

Other Subtle Signs of Emotional Immaturity

In addition to the three core behaviors above, emotionally immature individuals often display:

- **Passive-aggressiveness** instead of direct communication
- **Avoidance of hard conversations** (ghosting, stonewalling, shutting down)
- **Black-and-white thinking** (you're either "with them" or "against them")
- **Attention-seeking through drama** or emotional extremes
- A tendency to **expect others to meet all their emotional needs**

They often confuse **emotional expression** with **emotional responsibility** — believing that expressing a feeling is enough, without having to manage the consequences.

Where Does Emotional Immaturity Come From?

It' s easy to judge emotionally immature behavior — but it often has deep roots.

1. Unprocessed Childhood Dynamics

If someone grew up in a household where emotions were ignored, punished, or constantly dramatic, they may not have developed:

- Language for emotional expression
- Models for emotional regulation
- Safe environments to make mistakes and learn from them

2. Arrested Development

Some people experienced **trauma or instability** during key emotional development stages. Their emotional reactions stayed "stuck" at the age when the injury occurred.

3. Avoidance of Growth

For others, immaturity is not trauma-based — it's a choice. They simply **avoid the hard work of self-reflection**, and surround themselves with people who enable or excuse their behavior.

The Emotional Toll on Others

If you're in a relationship — romantic, professional, or familial — with an emotionally immature person, you may feel:

- **Exhausted from managing their reactions**
- **Gaslighted** into thinking you're always the problem
- **Resentful** because your needs are never prioritized
- **Trapped** in a cycle of apologies and false promises of change

You might find yourself apologizing for things you didn't do, or downplaying your own needs just to keep the peace.

Over time, this leads to **emotional burnout**, and a deep sense of being **unseen or unheard.**

How to Respond to Emotional Immaturity

If you're dealing with one:

- **Set clear emotional boundaries**
  "I'm willing to talk, but not if I'm being blamed for everything."
- **Don't play therapist**
  Their growth is not your job. You can offer compassion without becoming a cushion for bad behavior.
- **Watch for patterns, not promises**
  Many immature people say, *"I'll change,"* but what matters is repeated behavior.
- **Know when to walk away**
  If their emotional immaturity turns abusive, manipulative, or chronically neglectful — protect yourself.

If you recognize yourself:

- **Start by owning it**
  Emotional maturity begins the moment you stop blaming and start reflecting.
- **Practice regulation, not suppression**
  Learn to feel your feelings without exploding or shutting down.

- **Apologize and repair**
  When you hurt someone, take full accountability — without defending or justifying.

- **Stay teachable**
  You're allowed to evolve. Emotional maturity isn't about being perfect — it's about being **willing**.

It's not your fault if you weren't taught emotional maturity. But it is your responsibility to learn it.

Final Thought: Growing Up Is Emotional, Not Just Chronological

Being emotionally immature doesn't make someone bad. It makes them **unfinished** — still stuck in reflexes meant to avoid pain, not build connection.

You don't have to fix them. You don't have to stay for the chaos. But if you want to grow yourself, ask the hard question:

> *"Do I react, or do I respond? Do I blame, or do I build?"*

Because **emotional maturity isn't about never feeling big things** — it's about what you do with those feelings once they arrive.

How Quiet People Reveal Their Personality

They may not speak much — but if you know where to look, they're telling you everything.

Quiet people often go unnoticed — or misunderstood. In a world that celebrates loudness, charisma, and extroverted confidence, those who speak softly or sparingly are often labeled as shy, awkward, or aloof.

But that's rarely the whole story.

The truth is: **quiet doesn't mean empty.** Quiet people often have complex inner lives, strong values, and distinct personalities — they just express them through **subtler signals.**

So how do quiet people reveal who they really are?

You'll find the clues not in what they say, but in **how they respond, where they look, how they move, and when they finally speak**. Let's begin with one of the most overlooked yet powerful indicators:

People Who Are Embarrassed to Look Others in The Eye

Eye contact is often seen as a sign of confidence, but for quiet individuals, it can feel invasive. Many quiet people — especially those who are introspective, highly sensitive, or socially anxious — **avoid direct eye contact**, not because they're dishonest or disinterested, but because it feels emotionally intense.

What it looks like:

- Glancing quickly, then looking away
- Focusing on neutral spots (e.g., the table, their hands, the floor)
- Making brief eye contact only when speaking, not when listening
- Looking at your forehead or lips instead of your eyes

For some, eye contact feels like emotional exposure.

This doesn't mean they're lying or hiding. In fact, it may mean:

- They feel **emotionally flooded** in social situations
- They're deeply attuned to others' emotions, which makes eye contact **overwhelming**

- They grew up in environments where direct gaze felt unsafe or confrontational

Ironically, quiet people who avoid eye contact often **care more** than they appear — they're just trying not to drown in the emotional "noise" of interaction.

Stillness: A Form of Focus, Not Indifference

Quiet people often appear physically still. They sit without fidgeting. Their gestures are minimal. They rarely dominate physical space.

But this stillness isn't emptiness. It's often **internal activity** — they're processing, watching, evaluating.

What it means:

- Stillness is a form of **respectful listening**
- It reflects an ability to **tolerate silence**, rather than needing to fill it
- It often signals **emotional containment** — the ability to stay grounded, even in tense moments

Their calm presence isn't passivity. It's quiet regulation.

In group settings, the quiet person isn't disengaged — they're **filtering**. They're noticing who interrupts, who listens, and what's not being said.